Wings of Life

VEGETARIAN COOKERY BY JULIE JORDAN

*One day, almost three years ago, when I was cooking at the
MacDowell Artists Colony in Peterborough, New Hampshire,
I packed in the colonists' lunch baskets my favorite unyeasted
bread—an invention made from whole wheat flour, apricots,
raisins, bananas, yoghurt, and walnuts.*

A colonist, Tillie Olsen, sent me a note right back:

> *"Thanks for the bread—*
> *that's not staff of life bread—*
> *it's wings."*

The Crossing Press, Trumansburg, New York 14886

For Mom & Dad
who fed me—
and
For Uncle Bill

A Crossing Cookbook
Copyright © 1976, Julie Jordan
Cover & Title Page, David Sykes
Drawings of Fruits & Vegetables, Joanne Leary
Drawings of Cooking Tools, Steve Tetley
Kneading drawings & Chapter Border, Raymond Larrett

4th Printing—July 1978

Printed in the U.S.A.

Library of Congress Cataloging in Publication Data

Jordan, Julie.
  Wings of life.

  (A Crossing cookbook)
  Includes index.
  1. Vegetarian cookery. I. Title.
TX837.J57   641.5'636   76-43075
ISBN 0-912278-82-X
ISBN 0-912278-77-3

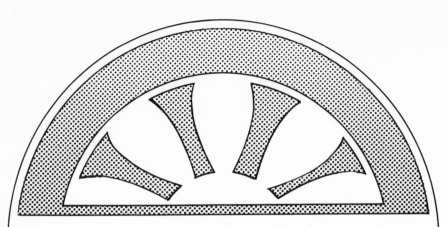

Contents

Introduction

There's a new kind of cooking—rising, bubbling, sprouting in our land. It's strong cooking, based solidly on foods the earth offers us. It's delicious cooking, flavored with the spices and traditional ingredients of many different cultures. But most of all, it's cooking bursting with creativity and genuine enjoyment of food.

The recipes in this book are all mine. The facts about food have been gleaned as part of my continuing search for the best foods possible and the best ways to prepare them. I was brought up by a food scientist father and a dietitian mother. I've been a home cook and a professional cook; a bread-baker; a glutton, a gourmet; a vineyard worker, a vegetable gardener. To satisfy my own curiosity, I've studied in the Graduate School of Nutrition at Cornell University. My life is an open-ended culinary experiment.

Using this book will be like having me with you—a teacher to encourage you and answer your questions, a friend with ideas.

I am a vegetarian. I stopped eating meat solely for convenience because I was living with vegetarians. After six months without meat, however, I realized I had become a vegetarian when I was invited out for Thanksgiving dinner and didn't want to eat the turkey. Since then, I've seen no reason to change. I like the taste of vegetarian foods. I like cooking without the grease and blood of meat. I like being completely detached from the slaughter of animals. As a vegetarian I feel cleaner, both physically and spiritually.

I have not eaten meat for five years and I am healthy. Numerous scientific studies show that an intelligently planned vegetarian diet is indeed nutritionally sound. The surest guide to health is to eat a wide variety of whole, natural foods. This guarantees that you'll receive the entire spectrum of nutrients (many of which are absent from processed foods) and that you will not receive any one nutrient in gross excess.

Processing and refining are overdone in our culture, and are definitely risky business. In highly refined foods many of the nutrients originally present are destroyed or removed, and only a few are added back in chemical equivalents. Several of the discarded vitamins and minerals are known to be essential, and fiber—present in whole grains, but missing from refined grains—is known to be necessary for regular elimination. Moreover, current research indicates that fiber is helpful in minimizing the risk of intestinal cancer and atheroscelerosis.

Vitamin pills will not compensate for the nutrients lost in refining, because they contain only a few nutrients. Furthermore, vitamin pills can give you an overdose of a specific vitamin, which may be just as dangerous as a deficiency.

Human beings do not know enough to replace food as a source of nutrients, and it will be a long time, if ever, before we will. Thank goodness.

Americans have a fixation on protein and consequently eat way too much of it. According to present U.S. recommended allowances, most American meat-eaters get about three times as much protein as they need. There is mounting scientific evidence that there may be a danger in eating too much protein. (Ammonia formed when excess protein is digested may cause mutations which lead to intestinal cancer.)

Protein is available in beans, grains, nuts, seeds, milk products, and eggs. There is no danger of vegetarians getting too little, and beginning vegetarians, rather than worrying about getting enough protein, should realize they're doing themselves a favor by cutting down. Statistics show, moreover, that American vegetarians eat about two times the protein they need, so even vegetarians should be careful not to eat too much concentrated protein food, such as eggs and cheese.

An additional reason for using moderation with eggs and cheese is their high fat and cholesterol content. By replacing meat with more grains, beans, and other vegetable products, vegetarians can decrease their intake of saturated fats and cholesterol, both of which have been implicated in problems of coronary heart disease. This advantage is offset if eggs and cheese are used too heavily.

The one nutrient a vegetarian might have to think about is iron, which meat-eaters get from the blood in meat and which old-time vegetarians probably got from dirt in their food. Today, with our ultra-clean food supply, vegetarians can be sure to get enough iron by choosing iron-rich foods such as dark green vegetables and dried fruits, and by cooking in cast iron pots. Some of the iron in these pots dissolves in the food you cook, and if your body needs it, this iron is available. (Iron you don't need is excreted.)

If you're interested in a vegetarian diet, but aren't used to vegetarian foods, don't make an overnight change. Sudden changes are bad for your body. Furthermore, unless the change is gradual, you will probably rebel against vegetarianism and go back to eating exactly what you did before. Instead, try eating a few vegetarian dishes, and as you find you like them, try increasing the variety.

Vegetarian breakfasts and lunches require no major changes in eating habits. Once you make homemade bread and granola, these meals will take care of themselves.

Dinner is the most challenging meal to plan, and it might take a while to get used to. Try sharing meals with vegetarian friends and eating at vegetarian restaurants, where someone else will select the meal for you. The Main Dishes chapter in this book presents recipes for substantial vegetarian main dishes and what to serve with them.

Don't panic if you've never heard of many of the ingredients in this book. Learning about them is an adventure. Besides, they're all readily available in supermarkets or at natural foods stores.

If you've never shopped at a natural foods store, take the first step and try one. The people there are part of the food movement and will help you.

Watch out for 'gimmick' health food stores, however. There are too many of them. You can usually tell a gimmick store by its walls lined with shelves of vitamin pills. These stores wrap food in tiny packages and charge you exorbitant prices.

If there's no natural foods store near you, I suggest ordering supplies from Walnut Acres, Penns Creek, Pa. 17862.

I recommend growing all the vegetables you possibly can yourself. Dig up your lawn. Find out about community garden plots. Small gardens are part of this food revolution. You'll not only be healthier if you get outside and garden, but every home-grown part of a meal will make it more delicious, fresher, and more special to cook and eat.

When gardening is impossible, find the local grocery store with the best produce counter. In some places there are farmers' markets, where you can buy locally grown produce. In cities, open air markets in the ethnic districts often carry fresh produce and other interesting ingredients. You can also join food co-ops, where you can buy vegetables and other supplies at reduced prices in return for helping with the work.

As you read this book, you'll find that I avoid blenders and other electrical equipment. In general I enjoy smashing and pounding things myself without the noise and wasted electricity of mechanical gadgets. I like getting exercise and being *hungry* after I cook. I also like lumps in my food: things too pasty smooth don't seem real.

My hand grain mill is my special love. With it I grind wheat berries to make flour for bread, pasta, and pie crusts. I grind rye berries into rye flour, corn into cornmeal, and dry bread into bread crumbs. I grind peanuts into peanut butter, and I grind fresh spices for curry powder. I recommend a hand grain mill as the most useful piece of kitchen equipment you can get. I also recommend a mortar and pestle for grinding up smaller quantities of herbs and spices.

I refuse to waste anything. This comes partly from a very frugal Norwegian heritage, and partly from a respect for what the earth provides. Mostly however, I enjoy synthesizing leftovers into exciting dishes, using potato water or yoghurt which didn't yoge to make bread. Whenever I bake bread, I cook beans and grains in the oven for future use. The oven is going, so I like to use its energy efficiently.

Wings Of Life is to help you discover vegetarian cooking and develop your own style.

Have fun.

Julia Jordan

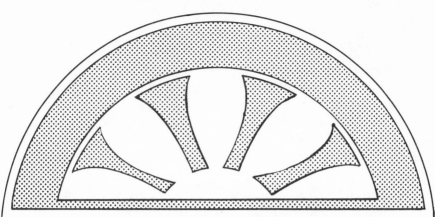

Bread Is Basic

Homemade bread is the heart of eating and the best part of cooking. I love mixing up dough, kneading and shaping loaves, smelling them bake, and sharing them with my friends. All the good feeling I want in food seems to rise with grainy bread.

SELECTING INGREDIENTS

Whole Wheat Flour

White flour can't hold a candle to whole wheat flour. Whole wheat flour is made by grinding or crushing whole wheat kernels, called wheat berries. The entire wheat kernel is there, just as the earth made it, with all the nutrients and natural taste.

To make white flour, the ground whole wheat powder is sifted and only the finest particles—those of the endosperm—are retained. The coarser particles of the bran and the germ of the wheat berry are discarded. You lose not only the taste and rich brownness of the whole grain flour, but also the nutrients of the bran and the germ. Enriching adds back chemical equivalents for some of the vitamins and minerals which are removed, but not all. Lost in the refining process are B vitamins, trace minerals, and fiber in the bran; Vitamin E, wheat germ oil, and B vitamins in the germ. A good deal of the protein of the wheat berry is also discarded, for it clings to the bran.

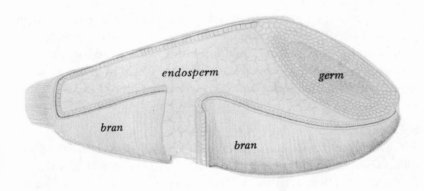

Unbleached white flour is just white flour with its slightly yellow natural color left in. Aside from eliminating the last refining step, bleaching, it's no better for you than bleached white flour. I see no reason to use it.

Whole wheat flour should be used fresh, because if it is kept for too long, the oils of the germ will go rancid. If you buy already-ground flour, I suggest you buy it in a natural foods store. Because of the problem of rancidity, many of the 'whole wheat flours' available in commercial stores are not true whole wheat. Most products in markets today require a long shelf life—true whole wheat flour will not keep.

In natural foods stores try to get *freshly ground flour.* Otherwise buy flour which seems to have a high turnover rate of sale; or buy flour which has been refrigerated.

The ideal way to guarantee freshness, however, is to *grind your flour yourself.* With a hand grain mill (which costs about twenty dollars for a steel wheel grinder or about forty dollars for a stone wheel), grinding flour is not only easy, but you'll know the whole wheat berry with all its nutrients will be in your flour. Fresh flour will give you a springy, lively dough to work with. And you'll taste the difference. (If you have a hand grain mill, you can buy whole wheat berries. Since they keep almost forever, you can purchase large quantities at a time and always have them on hand.)

Hard wheat
When buying wheat berries or flour for bread, try to find hard wheat varieties, especially hard red spring wheat. These have a high protein content, and hence make the most gluten—the springy protein network which traps air and holds your bread together. For this reason, flours made from hard wheat are said to give the 'strongest' doughs. Flour from hard wheat is called bread flour in stores.

Soft wheat
Soft wheat berries have less protein than hard wheat berries, so flours from them are not good for bread. However, soft wheat flours are excellent for making cakes, crêpes, and pie crusts, since you want them to be tender, rather than elastic. If you're looking for soft wheat flour in a store, it's usually called whole wheat pastry flour.

Liquids

Water

Water breads have a good grainy taste. Vegetable waters—the water
left after you steam vegetables—should always be saved. They
contain all the water-soluble vitamins (especially Vitamin C) lost
from the vegetables when they're cooked. Vegetable waters are
very good to use in bread, and potato water gives breads extra
body.

Milk

Milk breads have a charm, a mellowness you don't find in water
breads. They also keep fresh longer. I make milk breads on special
occasions or when someone I know has a milk cow. Raw milk has
the advantage of being fresh and of not being subjected to
extraneous processing. But since there is some risk of getting
undulant fever and other diseases, try to get milk from friends who
are careful with their cows, have their cows inspected, and drink
their milk themselves; or get milk from certified raw milk dairies.
I would advise against raw milk from any random cow.

If you buy commercial fluid milks, try to get un-modified,
un-Vitamin D fortified brands, as locally produced as possible.
Modified milks have more protein added, and this is a waste: there
is plenty of protein in milk to begin with. As for Vitamin D, it is a
nutrient which the human body produces itself when skin is
exposed to sunlight. (In fact many scientists think Vitamin D
shouldn't even be called a vitamin, since we don't need to eat it.)
If we concentrated on getting outside and getting some exercise,
we'd all be better off.

I very often buy non-fat dried milk powder. The non-instant kind
available in natural foods stores has not been modified, fortified
or enriched. It's excellent for making yoghurt, and mixed with
water makes good milk breads. If you ever reach this degree of
finesse, low-heat milk powders are best for yoghurt and high-heat
milk powders are best for baking. To make instant milk powder,
non-instant powder is moistened by steam until tiny particles stick
together in clusters. These clusters dissolve more easily.

Fats

Unrefined oils
Unrefined oils, even small amounts of them, add rich deep flavors to your cooking. My favorites for bread are corn germ oil and sesame oil. Refined oils are anonymous grease: they have all their taste processed out.

Store unrefined oils in cool places. They have no preservatives added to them; but the Vitamin E naturally present in the oils will prevent them from going rancid if they're kept cool.

Butter
I love nothing better than fresh bread spread with butter, and inside my loaves I use butter for a buttery rich taste. However, I try not to overdo butter, or fats in general, in my cooking. They carry a lot of calories, and are appreciated most when they're used sparingly, for their flavors.

Butter is a natural food. Margarine is a gross perversion of the natural vegetable oils from which it came. To make margarine, the unsaturated fats in the oils, which make oils liquid at room temperature, are artificially saturated to give margarine its solid texture. So margarine has the same saturated fat content as butter; and people who run to margarine to cut down on saturated fats are actually gaining nothing.

Honey

Honey is a precious ingredient. Nutritionally it's not much better for you than sugar, although it contains some minerals. But because it has taste and character, it encourages you to use it reverently in small amounts. This is as it should be: sweetness should be a surprise and a luxury.

Different honeys (from different kinds of flowers) are very distinct and add their own special flavors to your breads. Unheated, unfiltered honey is cloudy. It often crystallizes, unlike commercial pasteurized honeys. So look at the beauty of your unheated honey crystals rather than cursing how hard the honey is to pour.

Sea Salt

Sea salt is produced by evaporation of sea water. It contains an abundance of trace minerals (iodine in particular) which make it much superior to the pure sodium chloride of land-mined salt. Try to get gray, unrefined sea salt.

If you don't use sea salt, it's a good idea to use iodized salt. There are regions in the United States where there is no iodine in the soil, and people living in these regions, called the Goiter Belt, risk getting the iodine deficiency disease, goiter.

Yeast

I usually buy active dried yeast for making bread. Dried yeast granules contain a living but dormant yeast culture. You activate the microorganisms by dissolving the granules in warm water. Of the dried yeasts available, the kind in natural foods stores is the best. It is usually professional bakers' yeast and is fresh and vigorous. Kept cool in a well-sealed jar, it will stay peppy for a long time.

Compressed yeast cakes contain the same yeast culture, but the microorganisms have not been dried. Compressed yeast gives bread a wonderful yeasty taste. If you can buy the cakes fresh and use them rapidly, they're excellent for bread. For one tablespoon of dried yeast, substitute one small cake of compressed yeast or one-third of a big cake.

Bread was originally baked in flat cakes without yeast to raise it. Then, supposedly, an ancient Egyptian mixed a little fermenting wine into his bread dough, and when he left it overnight, he found that his dough puffed up. The yeast fermenting the wine, in addition to producing alcohol, produced carbon dioxide gas which leavened the bread. The dried or compressed yeast cakes we buy today are still near relatives of wine yeast.

Nutrition Fortifier Block

The nutrition fortifier block is an optional part of my bread recipe. It adds extra nutritive value to bread, gives it a special taste, a good texture, and helps keep it fresh longer. To each batch of bread (seven to eight cups of whole wheat flour), add

   1/2 cup non-fat dry milk powder
   1/2 cup soy flour
   2 tablespoons wheat germ
   2 tablespoons food yeast

Milk powder
This adds richness even if you don't use milk as the main liquid in your bread. It also adds calcium, protein, and B vitamins. And milk powder helps your crust brown.

Soy flour
The protein in soy flour complements the protein in whole wheat flour so both are more useful to your body. The lecithin in soy flour acts as a natural preservative. Bread made with part soy flour will stay fresh and moist longer. One-half cup of soy flour is two good-sized handfuls of soybeans ground up in your grain mill.

Wheat germ
Wheat germ is rich in Vitamin E and B vitamins. Be sure to add this if you have to buy commercial whole wheat flour. Keep wheat germ in the refrigerator so the oil in it will not go rancid.

Food (brewers') yeast
In the old days brewers' yeast was the dead yeast which settled to the bottom of the vats after beer was made. Today, special non-bitter cultures are grown for eating. It is dried out, and the resulting yeast is called food yeast. Since the yeast is dead, it cannot raise your bread.

Food yeast is the best source of B vitamins you can find, and an excellent source of iron. In baking and cooking, it gives a good, deep flavor.

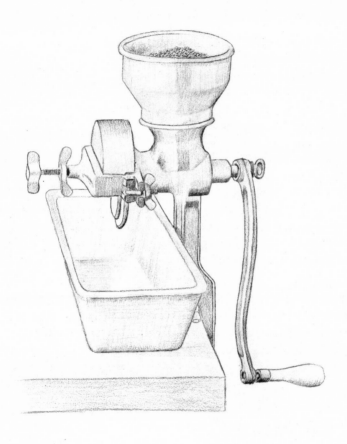

HAND GRAIN MILL—I grind grains fresh before I make bread.

GRAINY BREAD—DETAILED INSTRUCTIONS

Grainy bread is a wheaty, full-bodied bread with just a touch of honey. It's perfect for everything—for toast in the morning, for open face sandwiches, for buttering and eating with omelettes, for bread and cheese with soups and salads, and for serving with dinner. This recipe makes two big loaves or three little ones.

> 1 tablespoon dried yeast
> 1/2 cup wrist-temperature water
> 2 1/2 cups milk or water
> 2 tablespoons unrefined oil or butter
> 3 tablespoons honey
> 2 teaspoons sea salt
> Nutrition fortifier block (optional):
>> 1/2 cup non-fat dry milk powder
>> 1/2 cup soy flour
>> 2 tablespoons wheat germ
>> 2 tablespoons food yeast
> 7 to 8 cups (more or less) whole wheat flour

1. You always start making bread by dissolving your yeast to activate it. Stir it into 1/2 cup of water just so warm that you can't feel it when it's dripped on the underside of your wrist (the baby bottle test). Yeast likes body temperature or a little warmer, 105 to 110 degrees F. You have a few degrees to play around with, but water that is too hot will kill your yeast, and water that is too cold will leave it sleeping. Be careful and nothing will go wrong. Leave the yeast mixture to start bubbling in a separate cup while you go on to bowl operations.

2. If you're using milk for the bread liquid, heat it in a pot until it almost boils. This scalding not only destroys an enzyme in the milk which would inhibit gluten formation, but it also keeps the bread dough warm, which pleases your yeast no end. If you're using water, make sure it's hot. Pour the hot milk or water into a big bowl. I prefer crockery bread bowls because they stay warm.

3. Add the oil and honey. If you measure the oil first, it will coat the tablespoon and the honey won't stick as much. Swish the spoon in the hot milk or water to get every bit of honey off. Oil makes bread rich and moist. Honey makes it sweeter. Both help keep your bread fresh.

4. Measure in the salt. The cup of your palm is a perfect teaspoon. Try it, and salt flows out from your hand. Always add 2 teaspoons salt per batch of bread; without it, bread tastes flat.

5. Stir in the nutrition fortifier block (milk powder, soy flour, wheat germ, and food yeast), or as many of its ingredients as you're using. It doesn't matter if the milk powder doesn't dissolve: it will get worked in as you mix in flour.

6. Mix in well about 5 cups of whole wheat flour. If you've ground the flour fresh, it should be ground fine enough to feel silky. Three times through a hand grain mill, tightening down the grind each time, should do it. You can see the 3 parts of the wheat berry in the flour: the white endosperm is the bulk of the flour—It's called the middlings; the bran is darker; and the germ holds together in larger flaky pieces.

7. Remember the yeasty water from step 1? If the water is foamy, the yeast has been activated. Stir up the yeast mixture and pour it into the main bowl. As you gain experience, you very rarely lose yeast; but at the beginning there is a possibility. If your water is not foaming, you have 3 alternatives: take your chances and pour it in. Or stir it up and wait awhile to see if it might come around. Or suspect strongly that either your yeast was dead to begin with or that you killed it. Try dissolving a second batch and waiting. What if that doesn't work? You either find some new yeast fast, or turn to the Unyeasted Breads chapter.

8. Continue adding flour, about 1/2 cup at a time, stirring mightily after each addition. Stir in the same direction all the time to build up gluten.

You can watch the gluten forming. Those tiny stretching fibers are strands of gluten. They're made up of the proteins in the flour, which are kept separate from each other when the flour is dry. When you mix the flour with water and stir it, the proteins are brought together and begin to form the elastic gluten network.

The gluten will hold your bread together and give it the springy texture you're beginning to feel as you stir. Most importantly, when the yeast in your dough starts giving off carbon dioxide gas later, the gas will be trapped in pockets of gluten; they'll blow up like tiny balloons, causing your bread to rise.

The gluten strands in whole wheat bread can never get as long as those in white bread because the little flakes of bran in whole wheat flour have sharp edges and cut some of the gluten. If you look closely, you might be able to see that happening. Because bran cuts gluten, whole wheat bread is never as light and airy as white bread.

The more you stir, the more gluten will form, so don't be hesitant.

9. Add flour until you really can't stir any more. Then rub the dough off the spoon with your fingers, and plunge 1 hand into the bowl to start mixing. (You keep the other hand dry so you can add more flour with it.) The dough should be warm and sticky.

10. Mix in flour with your hand until the dough starts to hold together in a ball and leave the sides of the bowl. The best way to mix the dough is to sweep in one direction around the bowl in order to keep the gluten strands whole.

11. Lift the dough onto a floured bread board or counter. Pour a little flour into your bread bowl and rub it around with your fingers to pick up any bits of dough that might have stuck. Add the bits to the main bulk of the dough. While you still have a clean hand, pour a little oil into the bread bowl for use in step 14.

12. Now wait a few minutes to let your dough rest. The proteins in the flour will absorb more water, your dough won't take up as much new flour when you knead it, and your loaf will be lighter.

13. Start kneading. This is the heart of bread-baking, when you and your bread push together, thump together. Kneading is such a relaxing experience that, even if you start in the foulest mood, by the time you finish kneading you'll feel at peace with the world again. Whenever you feel tense, making bread is guaranteed to cure you.

To knead, fold the dough in half towards you—your right hand folding, your left hand pushing the dough in the center to help.

1 Push dough down & away from you.

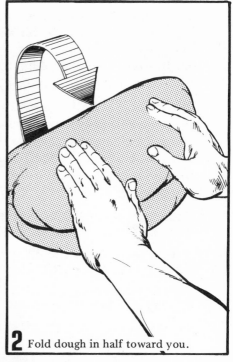

2 Fold dough in half toward you.

3 Push dough down & away from you.

(Left-handed people reverse the hands.) With the heels of both your palms on the edge of the dough nearest you, push the dough down and away from you. Retrieve the dough, put a little more flour on the board if the dough sticks, then turn the dough 90 degrees and fold again. This process gets smooth, rhythmic. Watch your friends knead. It's beautiful.

Kneading builds up still more gluten than you've worked up by stirring; and kneading lines up the gluten strands to form the strong framework of pockets which will hold in the gas given off by the yeast. You can feel your dough getting more elastic as you knead and more gluten develops.

After 5 to 10 minutes of kneading with a good rhythm, your bread ball will almost stop taking up flour, and will spring back slowly when you poke your thumb in it. That's it for kneading. Store any flour you have left over in an airtight container in a cool place. (When I grind flour, I usually grind too much just so I won't run out half-way through kneading.)

Adding all your flour and kneading your dough like this before the first rising is called the 'straight rise' method. I prefer it because I like the entire creative process to occur at once. The other major method of making bread is the 'sponge rise' method, in which you let your dough rise once with only part of the flour mixed into it.

14. Put the ball of dough back into your oiled bread bowl, and spin it around to give it a coating of oil. Then turn the ball over so the oily side is up. This helps keep the dough from drying out. Cover the bowl with a clean damp towel.

15. Search out a warm spot and leave the bread there to rise. In the summer warm spots are easy to find. Wet the towel every now and then because the sun will dry it out. In the winter, the furnace top, water heaters, and radiators are warm. Spots near wood-burning stoves are God's gift to bread yeast. Above the pilot light of a gas stove is also good. Or you can light your oven to heat it up to about 200 degrees F, then turn it off and shove in your bread bowl. (A pan of boiling water in the bottom of the oven will keep it warm longer.) Or fill your sink with hot water and float the bread bowl in it.

If you give yeast a warm damp atmosphere, it will grow and reproduce. To get energy it will ferment the sugars from the honey and from the breakdown of the starch in the flour. As by-products of this fermentation, it will give off carbon dioxide gas which will raise your bread, and alcohol which evaporates away in baking. This yeast fermentation is a living process. Keep your yeast warm, moist, and well-fed, and it will work for you.

16. About 1 to 1 1/2 hours later, when your yeast will have released enough carbon dioxide gas to raise the dough up to double its original size, punch your dough solidly in the middle. It's enormously satisfying to let go with a really good wallop every now and then. Watch the dough deflate around your fist as all the carbon dioxide puffs out. Fold the edges of the dough into the center to squeeze out air bubbles. These first bubbles are large and uneven in size. The popping and stretching divide up the bubbles and help make your final bread much more even-textured.

17. You can shape your bread now; but it's best to cover it with a damp towel, return it to its warm spot, and let it rise again. The second rising will take only 45 minutes to an hour.

18. Now that your dough has doubled in bulk a second time, get ready to shape it. Oil or butter your bread board a little to keep your loaves from sticking. Butter your bread pans, bottom and sides. Butter is better than oil for pans because it sticks to the sides of the pan. Oil slides down, and your bread will come out in pieces despite all your intricate prying. For this much dough I use either two 9-5/8x5-1/2 inch pans (standard loaf pans) or three 7-5/8x3-3/4 inch pans (smaller pans with the same loaf shape). You can also butter a flat baking tray and make lots of rolls.

19. Punch down the dough and place it on the oiled board. Cut the dough with a knife into the number of loaves you want. Then shape each piece of dough to fit its pan. Try to work out large air bubbles as you shape by pressing the dough on the bread board. Try not to tear the dough, as that will break up the gluten. Never work in flour at this point: it won't dissolve and will coarsen your bread. Slip each loaf into its pan when you finish shaping it.

20. You can jazz up the crusts now if you want to. Slash them. Carve letters on them. Paint them with a beaten egg for a golden glazed crust; or with milk for a rich brown crust; or with melted butter for a soft butter crust. Sprinkle sesame seeds or poppy seeds on them. Both kinds of seeds together look exotic. Or don't do anything. A plain crust is fine too.

21. Here's the last rising. Put your loaves—now in pans—back in their warm spot. The damp cloth would stick to them, so leave them uncovered. Let the loaves rise for 30 minutes. They won't necessarily be doubled in bulk this time.

22. Preheat the oven to 425 degrees F. Slide in your loaves. The high oven temperature sears over the surface of the loaves. On the inside, the yeast is still alive and continues releasing gas into the pockets in the loaves. This keeps the inside of the loaves rising up firm against the crust.

23. After 15 minutes at 425 degrees F, turn the oven down to 350 degrees F. The insides of the loaves will be hot now, and having accomplished its mission, the yeast will die. The loaves will stay risen because, during the rest of the baking, steam from the liquids in the bread will fill the gas pockets, and gradually the gluten strands forming the pockets will stiffen until they can stand up on their own. The crust of the bread will be turning golden brown during this time. Browning is due mostly to the proteins and sugars on the surface of the loaf reacting together because of the heat. (This process makes toast brown too.)

24. Check your loaves after 20 minutes at 350 degrees F. They probably won't look done. If they do, however, take 1 loaf out of the oven and tip it out of its pan. Tap it on the bottom. If it sounds hollow, it's done. If it isn't done, put it back in the oven and check everything again 10 minutes later. There's a greater, in fact a very good chance of your loaves being done now. Tap each loaf. Bigger ones take longer to cook than little ones; ovens bake unevenly too. So trust your own judgment rather than following the times given in the recipe religiously.

Tip each loaf out of its pan. If you want a really soft crust, brush the tops of the loaves with butter while they're piping hot. Then leave the loaves on cooling racks to cool with air circulating around them. This is a friendly time. The smell of fresh-baked bread will draw everyone into the kitchen.

You've done it!

Let the bread which doesn't get devoured immediately cool off completely. Then store it unwrapped in a bread box: a good air crust will keep bread fresher than anything you could wrap it in.

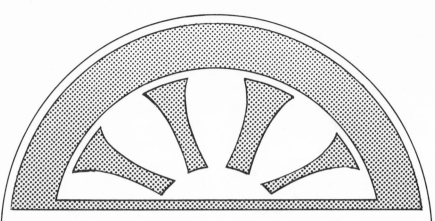

Other Yeasted Breads

When you've made grainy bread a few times and feel comfortable, begin to experiment. You'll enjoy baking most and you'll make your best bread if you improvise and try out your own ideas. Even if some loaves don't come out the way you intended, all is not lost: grainy breads have a way of tasting delicious no matter what you do to them.

VARIATIONS ON STANDARD GRAINY BREAD

Other Flours

Once you've added five cups of whole wheat flour and have stirred up gluten, you can start adding different flours. Always use five cups of whole wheat flour first, because no other flour can form the gluten network which is necessary for bread to rise. I think breads made from part rye flour have more character than pure whole wheat breads. They're slightly darker and more flavorful. Rye flour contains the proteins to make gluten, but since it also contains a gummy material which inhibits gluten formation, breads made with part rye flour are always denser than pure whole wheat breads. Oatmeal and cornmeal give excellent tastes to bread, especially when molasses is used for sweetening.

Liquids

Instead of using milk or water, I often use yoghurt, sour milk or buttermilk. These do not need to be scalded. To make breads with a real Scandinavian taste, try using sour milk. (Leave out the honey and cut down on the salt.)

All vegetable waters make excellent breads. Potato water is the traditional liquid in rye bread, giving it a satisfying flavor and moistness. Sweet potato water and mashed sweet potatoes, with extra molasses added, give golden and slightly sweet loaves. The first soaking water from your seeds when you are making sprouts contains some of the water-soluble vitamins from the seeds, and is a fine liquid to use in breads.

Two or three eggs add richness to loaves of grainy bread. Beat the eggs lightly in a separate bowl and add them to the bread liquid. Wait until the liquid is slightly cool so the eggs don't cook as you beat them in.

Grains—Cooked & Uncooked

I almost always add cooked grains to my bread dough, since they give loaves a springy feel and keep the bread fresh longer. I use whatever cooked grains I have on hand stored in the refrigerator. Cooked brown rice, millet, wheat berries, barley, and oats are all good. I add two or three cups of cooked grains to the bread liquid.

Cracked wheat is the best uncooked grain. I make it by running wheat berries through my grain mill once on a coarse grind. Mix one cup of cracked wheat into the bread dough after you've stirred up gluten, and it will make chewy little morsels.

Herbs & Onions

Herb and vegetable breads are my favorites. Deep, savory tastes go well with the yeast flavor. For a two-loaf batch of bread, stir two to three teaspoons of dried herbs into the liquid. Sage, marjoram, thyme, rosemary, dill, and basil—each alone or several mixed together—make the kinds of breads you eat with cheese, or with soups and salads. Caraway, anise, and fennel seeds, or any combination, are delicious in rye bread.

Onion breads are out of this world. Chop up two or three onions, then mix them into your bread liquid. You can also cook the onions in butter before you add them. Caraway and dill seeds are good in onion bread.

Raw celery and green peppers are good chopped up in bread. Raw carrots and parsnips should be grated. Sprouts make a sweet, pleasant crunch. When you add vegetables to bread, because of their extra volume it's a good idea to add about one-half teaspoon extra of salt per two-loaf batch of bread.

Dried Fruits, Seeds, & Spices

Breads with a sweet theme are good for breakfast or snacks and to eat with nut butters. Mix raisins, dates, and dried currants into your bread liquid to make little pockets of sweetness. To make the dough sweet too, add more honey, molasses or maple syrup than I specify in the standard grainy bread recipe. Sunflower seeds and poppy seeds are good added to sweet breads, as are all kinds of nuts. Grated orange rind, or about one teaspoon of cinnamon are unusual tastes.

In the following recipes in this chapter, the nutrition fortifier block is an optional addition.

Cinnamon Rolls

A sweet treat. Cinnamon, honey, raisins, and walnuts are swirled together in a tender dough with a gorgeous sticky glaze. Serve with butter and coffee for breakfast or brunch.

Dough:
- 1 tablespoon dried yeast
- 1/2 cup wrist-temperature water
- 2 1/2 cups milk, scalded
- 1/4 cup butter
- 1/2 cup honey
- 2 teaspoons sea salt
- 2 eggs, lightly beaten
- 7 to 8 cups (more or less) whole wheat flour

Filling:
- 1 cup honey
- 4 teaspoons cinnamon
- 4 to 6 handfuls raisins
- 4 to 6 handfuls walnuts, in big pieces

Glaze:
- 1/2 cup butter, melted
- 1/2 cup honey
- 1 teaspoon cinnamon

1. Make up the bread dough and let it rise the first 2 times as for grainy bread.
2. Mix together the ingredients for the filling.
3. When you're ready to shape the dough, divide it in half. With a rolling pin, roll each half into a rectangle, 9x18 inches, about 1/4 inch thick.
4. Spread each piece of dough with half the filling mixture. Roll up each piece lengthwise and cut it into slices 1/2 inch thick.
5. Mix up the glaze, and use it to cover the bottom of four 9 inch round cake pans, two 9x13 inch rectangular baking pans, or any combination of pans you choose.
6. Arrange the slices in the glaze. Lay them out flat so they're just touching each other.
7. Let the rolls rise 1/2 hour in a warm spot. Bake them in a 400 degrees F oven for about 15 minutes, or until their tops start to brown.

8. Tip the rolls out of the pans onto plates or trays immediately when you remove them from the oven. The glaze will cover the rolls smoothly.

Yield: 3 dozen rolls

Oatmeal Bread

A sweet and delicious 'gobble-me-up' bread. Oats give it a heart, a real home-baked taste. Good spread with butter and sliced ripe tomatoes.

1 tablespoon dried yeast
1/2 cup wrist-temperature water
2 1/2 cups potato water or milk
1/4 cup butter
1/4 cup honey
1/4 cup molasses
2 teaspoons sea salt
5 cups whole wheat flour
2 cups rolled oats, soaked in 1 cup boiling water
3 to 4 cups (more or less) whole wheat flour

Follow directions in the Bread Is Basic chapter.

Yield: 2 loaves

Pumpernickel

Pumpernickel is a dark moist rye bread with plenty of caraway seeds. Use it for open face sandwiches.

    1 tablespoon dried yeast
    1/2 cup wrist-temperature water
    2 1/2 cups potato water
    2 tablespoons unrefined oil
    1/2 cup molasses
    1 tablespoon sea salt
    1 tablespoon caraway seeds
    5 cups whole wheat flour
    2 to 3 cups (more or less) rye flour

Follow directions in the Bread Is Basic chapter.

Yield: 2 loaves

Filled Pumpernickel Roll

Pumpernickel dough filled with a mixture of sautéed onions, mushrooms, and sour cream.

    Filling:
        1 large onion, diced
        1/4 pound mushrooms, sliced
        1 cup sour cream
        2 pinches salt

1. Make pumpernickel dough and let it rise the first 2 times.
2. Meanwhile sauté the onion and mushrooms until tender in a little butter. Cool and mix them with the sour cream and salt.
3. When the dough is ready to shape, divide it in half. Shape 1 half as a normal loaf. With a rolling pin, roll the other half into a large rectangle. Spread the dough with the filling, roll it up, and fit it into a bread pan.
4. Let the 2 breads rise 1/2 hour in the pans. Then bake them as usual—15 minutes at 425 degrees F, then about 20 to 25 minutes more at 350 degrees F.

Yield: 1 filled loaf and 1 loaf plain pumpernickel

Carrot Cheese Bread

Golden loaves flaked with orange carrots. Firm and slicable for sandwiches. Toast and spread it with butter to bring out the cheese flavor.

1 tablespoon dried yeast
1/2 cup wrist-temperature water
2 1/2 cups milk, scalded
2 tablespoons butter
3 tablespoons honey
1 tablespoon sea salt
2 teaspoons ground coriander
3 large carrots, grated
1/2 pound Cheddar cheese, grated
8 to 9 cups (more or less) whole wheat flour

Follow directions in the Bread Is Basic chapter.

Yield: 2 loaves

Double Dill Bread

A light dill rye bread. One of my favorites for breakfast, with honey and thin slices of Swiss cheese.

1 tablespoon dried yeast
1/2 cup wrist-temperature water
1 1/2 cups hot water
1 cup yoghurt
2 tablespoons unrefined oil or butter
3 tablespoons honey
2 teaspoons sea salt
1 tablespoon dried dill weed
1 tablespoon dill seed
1 tablespoon caraway seed
5 cups whole wheat flour
3 cups (more or less) rye flour

Follow directions in the Bread Is Basic chapter.

Yield: 2 loaves

Herb & Butter Bread

Fragrant of herbs as you mix and bake it. A natural with dinner.

 1 tablespoon dried yeast
 1/2 cup wrist-temperature water
 2 1/2 cups milk, scalded
 1/2 cup butter
 1/4 cup honey
 2 teaspoons sea salt
 1 teaspoon dried basil
 1 teaspoon caraway seeds
 1/4 teaspoon dried thyme
 7 to 8 cups (more or less) whole wheat flour

Follow directions in the Bread Is Basic chapter.

Yield: 2 loaves

Savory Bread

An onion bread with a hearty taste. My favorite version of grainy bread.

 1 tablespoon dried yeast
 1/2 cup wrist-temperature water
 2 1/2 cups hot water (Vegetable water is best.)
 2 tablespoons unrefined oil
 3 tablespoons honey
 1 tablespoon sea salt
 2 or 3 medium onions, finely chopped
 2 cups cooked brown rice
 5 cups whole wheat flour
 3 to 4 cups (more or less) rye flour

Follow directions in the Bread Is Basic chapter.

Variations:
—Along with the onions, add chopped green pepper, chopped celery, grated carrots, or sprouts.
—Substitute cooked barley for rice and add 2 teaspoons thyme.
—1 tablespoon caraway seeds or dill seeds complements the onion to give a totally new taste.

Yield: 2 loaves

Whole Wheat Challah

Challah, the traditional Jewish egg bread, is shaped in a big braid, and is probably the most stunning-looking loaf you can make.

1. Add 4 eggs to a 2-loaf batch of standard grainy bread dough. (See the Bread Is Basic chapter.)
2. After the dough has risen a second time, punch it down, and divide it in half to make 2 loaves. To shape 1 loaf, cut the dough into 3 pieces, and roll each out to a long snake. Fasten the 3 snakes together at one end. Then braid them as you would braid hair. Slip the braid onto a buttered baking tray. Repeat with the other half of the dough.
3. Let the braids rise for 1/2 hour in a warm spot. Brush them with beaten egg for a glaze, and sprinkle them with poppy or sesame seeds.
4. Bake as you would grainy bread.

Yield: 2 braided loaves

Brown Rice Bagels

Bagels have the satisfying bagel chew, enhanced here by brown rice. I like toasted bagel halves with cream cheese and sliced tomatoes.

1. Add 2 cups cooked brown rice to a 2-loaf batch of standard grainy bread dough. (See the Bread Is Basic chapter.)
2. After the dough has risen a second time, punch it down. Cut it into pieces the size of good apples, and roll each piece into a smooth ball. Stick your thumb through the center of each ball to make a tire, then squiggle your thumb around to enlarge the hole.
3. Let the tires rise for 1/2 hour in a warm spot. Then drop them 3 at a time into a pot of boiling water, and cook until they rise to the surface.
4. Take the bagels out of the water, letting them drip off. Arrange them on a buttered baking sheet.
5. Brush a beaten egg glaze over the bagels. Then leave them plain or sprinkle them with sesame seeds, poppy seeds, or bits of minced onion.
6. Bake in a 425 degrees F oven for about 20 to 30 minutes, or until the bagels are crusty and brown.

Yield: 20 bagels

EXOTIC BREADS

Wheat Soy French Bread

My version of French bread is long, golden-brown, and crusty. It's not real French bread, since that cannot be made with whole wheat flour. Gluten is the key in French-style bread. With the no-knead method used here, instead of kneading the dough to build up the gluten framework, you let the dough rise several times and the dough works up gluten by itself. You also leave out the oil and honey to facilitate gluten formation.

One of the prime delights of wheat soy French bread is its natural affinity for soft ripened cheeses (like Brie and Camembert) and wine. Some of the most enjoyable meals of my life have been based on those three foods and the company of friends. If you put French bread in a basket on the table, people can break off pieces to butter as they talk. If you cut wheat soy French bread into cubes, it's perfect for dipping into cheese fondue because the crust holds the cubes together when you spear them. Wheat soy French bread is also delicious for breakfast with butter and thin slices of Norwegian gjetost (a brown goats' milk cheese).

    1 tablespoon dried yeast
    1/2 cup wrist-temperature water
    2 1/2 cups hot water
    2 teaspoons sea salt
    5 cups whole wheat flour
    1 cup soy flour
    1 cup (more or less) whole wheat flour

1. In a separate cup dissolve the dried yeast in 1/2 cup wrist-temperature water.
2. Pour the hot water into your bread bowl, and stir in the salt.
3. Sift in through a strainer 5 cups of whole wheat flour, about 1 cup at a time, stirring well after each addition. Save all the coarse bran flakes which don't sift through.
4. Add the yeast water from step 1 and mix it in well.
5. Stir in the bran and the soy flour, then sift in about 1/2 cup more whole wheat flour and stir it in.

36/Other Yeasted Breads

6. The dough will be sticky, but stop adding flour anyway. Just stir and stir for about 3 minutes or until your arm gives out. (I rest a little after every minute stirring; and this actually is good because it gives the gluten proteins time to pick up more water.) Stir in the same direction all the time to work up the best gluten.

7. Cover the bowl with a damp towel, and leave it in a warm spot until it doubles in bulk, about 1 1/2 hours.

8. Punch down the dough, fold its edges into the center, and let it rise again, this time for about 1 hour.

9. Punch. Notice how the dough is getting more elastic, less sticky. You can see very long strands of gluten forming. Rise again, for about 45 minutes to 1 hour.

10. Punch. Rise for about 45 minutes to 1 hour.

11. Punch down the dough for the last time. Knead it on a floured counter for about 2 or 3 minutes. You may knead in up to 1/2 cup more flour here if you feel your dough needs it. (How much extra flour you'll require depends on the type of flour you've used. Flours with the most protein take up the most water.)

12. Cut the dough in half or in thirds, and roll each portion into a long cylinder to make a French-shaped loaf.

13. Put the loaves on baking sheets sprinkled with cornmeal and let the loaves rise for 1/2 hour in a warm spot.

14. Preheat the oven to 425 degrees F and put a pan of boiling water in the bottom for steam. Slash the tops of the loaves with a very sharp knife or a razor blade, and brush or spray the loaves with water. (A perfume atomizer is perfect for spraying.) Put the loaves immediately in the oven.

15. Bake 15 minutes at 425 degrees F, then turn down the oven to 350 degrees F and bake 20 to 25 minutes more. Open the oven door and spray in more water occasionally.

16. The loaves are done if they're golden and hard when you tap them. Slide them immediately onto cooling racks so they'll stay crusty.

For the real French touch, line 1 shelf in your oven with unglazed ceramic tiles (available at some hardware or building supply stores). Put your loaves to rise on a wooden board sprinkled with cornmeal instead of on baking sheets. Then when the loaves are ready to bake, slide them off the board directly onto the tiles in the oven. You get a terrific bottom crust this way.

Yield: 2 or 3 long French-style loaves

Arabic Bread (Pita)

Arabic bread comes in soft rounds which look almost like large pancakes with air pockets. The trick is to get the air pockets.

To eat Arabic bread, cut a round in half with a sharp knife. Puffed up breads can be pried open gently with your fingers, and you have a pocket for stuffing. Even if a round hasn't puffed up completely, once you cut it in half, you can pry it open with a sharp knife. Stuff the pockets with salads or luscious Middle Eastern fillings like hummus or baba ganoush, or with lettuce, cheese, tomatoes, and tahini. Sandwiches in pockets of Arabic bread are perfect for lunch. They're especially handy for little kids because nothing falls out of them. You can also use Arabic bread as pincers to pick up tabbouleh, baba ganoush or hummus.

> 1 tablespoon dried yeast
> 1/2 cup wrist-temperature water
> 2 1/2 cups hot water (Vegetable water is best.)
> 2 tablespoons olive oil
> 2 teaspoons sea salt
> 5 cups whole wheat flour
> 1/2 cup soy flour
> 3 to 4 cups (more or less) whole wheat flour

1. In a separate cup dissolve the dried yeast in 1/2 cup wrist-temperature water.
2. Mix together the hot water, oil, salt, and about 5 cups whole wheat flour in your bread bowl.
3. Pour in the yeasty water, and stir it up.
4. Mix in the soy flour, then continue adding whole wheat flour until the dough is ready to knead.
5. Knead the dough a good 10 minutes. You want really well-developed gluten.
6. Oil your bread bowl with olive oil, and put the dough back in. Cover it with a damp cloth and leave it to rise in a warm spot until doubled in bulk—about 1 1/2 hours. (Up to this point making Arabic bread is very similar to making grainy bread.)
7. Now punch down the dough. Cut it into 12 equal pieces with a sharp knife. Roll each piece into a ball. Then arrange the balls on a floured counter and leave them to rest for about 1/2 hour.

8. On a lightly floured counter, roll 6 of the balls out into 7 inch or 8 inch rounds with a rolling pin. Arrange them so they aren't touching each other on baking sheets sprinkled with cornmeal. (Try to keep the cornmeal just under the rounds of bread. Cornmeal lying on the baking sheet between rounds burns in the hot oven. It causes no harm, but the extra cornmeal blackening fills your kitchen with smoke.)

9. Put the rounds on the trays back in the warm spot to rise for 1/2 hour. During this rising, air pockets will form in the dough. You'll bake the risen rounds at a very high temperature so the air in these pockets will expand suddenly. The dough will still be soft, so the expanding air will puff it up like magic.

10. While your first rounds are rising, roll out the remaining balls of dough. They'll rise while you're cooking the first batch.

11. Preheat the oven to 500 degrees F. The high oven temperature is crucial to success.

12. Bake the breads, one baking sheet at a time. If you have a gas oven, bake the bread on the floor of the oven for 5 minutes, then move the baking sheet to a shelf about 4 inches above the oven floor, and continue baking for 3 to 4 minutes until the puffy rounds are a delicate brown. Try not to overcook them on top. You want them to be soft and blousy when you take them out, not brittle. If you have an electric oven, bake the bread on the lowest shelf for 5 minutes, then move the baking sheet up to the next shelf and bake the breads 3 to 4 minutes more.

13. After you bake the breads on each sheet, remove them and pop them into an airtight container such as a biscuit tin, or if you don't have one of those, put them in a paper bag. The warm breads will steam, and the steam will keep them soft. Although the puffs will collapse, there will be a nice air pocket left in the center.

14. Continue baking all the rounds, popping them in the biscuit tin when they're done.

15. Remove all the rounds from the tin in 10 minutes so they don't get soggy.

Yield: 12 round breads

Sourdough Starter

If you'd like to make sourdough bread and don't have a starter, I'd recommend finding friends who have one and asking them to divide it, or buying a dried sourdough culture, or making your own. Here's a recipe for sourdough starter.

1 tablespoon dried yeast
2 cups warm water
2 cups rye flour

1. Mix together the ingredients in a non-metal bowl.
2. Cover the bowl with a plate. Leave the mixture for 3 days at room temperature until it's bubbly and sour.

The microorganisms in homemade starters are more random than those in a bought culture, so breads made from homemade starters, although good, are usually a bit harsher than those from commercial starters. You can tell a lot about the tastes your bread will have from the smell of your starter.

Keep your starter in a covered crock or in a loosely covered glass jar. (A clip-top canning jar is good.) If you use the culture every few days, you can leave it out at room temperature and the culture will be very lively. If you use it less often, keep it in the refrigerator so the microorganisms will grow less quickly. It's good to keep a bit more than 2 cups of starter in the jar so you never use more than half your culture at once.

Whenever you make sourdough bread, stir up your starter and use 1 cup of it. Build the starter back to its original volume by mixing in equal parts of whole wheat flour and warm water. This gives the microorganisms new food so they can keep growing.

If you haven't used your starter in a very long time—say a month—pour it out of its jar into a bowl, feed it with a little flour and water, and leave it out at room temperature to give the microorganisms a boost. Then clean the jar and pour the starter back. (Clean the jar occasionally even if you use the starter regularly.)

If you take care of it—feed it, clean its house, and exercise it—your sourdough starter will stay fresh and peppy for years.

Sourdough Bread

The pure, fresh-grain sourdough taste. And what a crust! This is an extraordinary recipe.

    1 cup sourdough starter
    1 1/2 cups warm water
    1 tablespoon honey
    1 teaspoon sea salt
    4 cups whole wheat flour
    1 teaspoon baking soda
    1 to 2 cups (more or less) whole wheat or rye flour

1. Mix together the starter, water, honey, salt, and 4 cups of whole wheat flour. Cover the bowl with a plate or a damp cloth. Let the sponge sit for 12 to 18 hours in a warm spot. The longer you let it sit, the more sour your final dough will be.
2. After 12 to 18 hours, mix in the baking soda and 1 cup of whole wheat or rye flour. Continue mixing in flour a little at a time until the dough is ready to knead.
3. Knead 5 to 10 minutes.
4. Put the dough back in its lightly oiled bowl, cover it, and return it to its warm spot. Let it sit for 6 hours.
5. Punch down the dough and shape it. Sourdough does not like to be shaped in bread pans. Either shape a big round loaf or 2 long thin loaves. Put them on a baking tray sprinkled with cornmeal.
6. Let the loaves sit for another 6 hours in the warm spot.
7. Preheat the oven to 425 degrees F, and put a pan of boiling water in the bottom for steam. Slash the loaves with a very sharp knife or a razor blade. Brush them with salt water.
8. Put the loaves into the oven, or slide them off the tray onto an oven shelf lined with unglazed ceramic tiles. Bake 15 minutes at 425 degrees F. Then turn the oven down to 350 degrees F and bake the loaves 25 to 30 minutes more or until they're done. They will sound hollow when they're tapped on the bottom. Brush the loaves again with salt water about 5 minutes before you finally remove them from the oven.

Yield: 1 big round loaf or 2 long thin loaves

Uses For Stale Bread

If by some strange twist of fate, your bread doesn't get eaten right away and you have old bread around, you have the rare opportunity of making fondue, croutons, or bread crumbs.

Bread for cheese fondue
When bread just starts to dry out, cut it into cubes, spear the cubes, and dip them into cheese fondue. All kinds of bread are good for fondue. (See Index)

Croutons
Cut your old bread into small cubes. Leave them out in the air to dry completely if you want. Mash a clove of garlic in salt. In a skillet mix the garlic salt with about one tablespoon of olive oil. Add the bread cubes and fry them, shaking them around in the pan to get them brown all over.

Toss croutons into salads for a delicious savory crunch. Do it at the very last minute so they stay crisp. Croutons are especially good in spinach salads.

Bread crumbs
Break up your old bread and leave it out in the air until it's bone-dry. If you're using the oven, you can even dry the bread pieces in the oven on a tray. Then grind them through your grain mill or a meat grinder on a very coarse grind.

Bread crumbs are great things to have. Stuff zucchini with crumbs, cheese, and herbs. Sprinkle crumbs on all your casseroles with snipped-up fresh parsley. Or, best of all, make my Mom's macaroni and cheese.

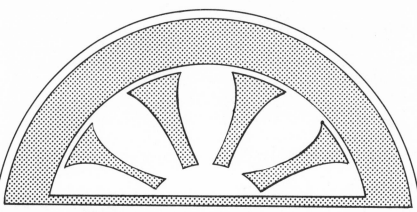

Unyeasted Breads

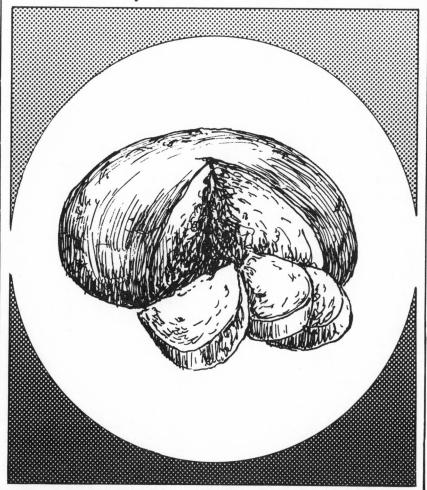

More than any other food, unyeasted breads are my soul's dish, my symphony, my book of no-nonsense philosophy. I like unyeasted breads because they're solid and unpretentious, dark-brown and earthy, and when you bite into them, there's really something there.

Unyeasted breads place no demands on you. Unhindered by any expectation that your loaves should rise, you can mix in anything you want. You can give vent to your fondness for fennel, your passion for peanuts. You can knead to your heart's content. You can be courageous.

GENERAL RECIPE

Bread started out in ancient times as a kind of cake, made of water, meal or flour—mostly from barley and millet—honey, oil, sweet wine, cooked grains, and fruits. The Hebrews, Chinese, and Egyptians introduced flat cakes made from a flour and water dough. They used wheat flour and discovered that kneading worked up gluten and held the bread together. And, aside from a digression into yeasted bread-making, here we are now. Unyeasted bread is still with us. And it's still liquids and solids—mostly flour; it has some surprises thrown in; then it's mixed together, kneaded, and baked.

1. Pour liquids into your bread bowl. They can be any liquids you want to use, potato or other vegetable water, yoghurt that failed to yoge, mashed ripe bananas. You can also start with good old milk or water. About 3 cups of liquid makes a good amount of dough to knead—2 loaves' worth.

2. Add 1/4 cup unrefined oil. Try different kinds—sesame, peanut, corn germ oil. All are rich and softening.

3. Add 1/4 cup honey. You might also try molasses or maple syrup for different sweet tastes.

4. Add 1 tablespoon (= 3 teaspoons = 3 palmfuls) of sea salt.

5. I often add the same nutrition fortifier block I use for yeasted breads.

> 1/2 cup non-fat dry milk powder
> 1/2 cup soy flour
> 2 tablespoons wheat germ
> 2 tablespoons food yeast

6. Mix in solids, any shape or flavor, your leftovers, your treasures. Chewy cooked grains—brown rice, millet, rye berries, wheat berries—are sources of B vitamins, protein, and minerals. Dried fruits are almost a must in unyeasted breads, providing a deep moist sweetness. They're also good sources of iron, and are very important in our diets. Use raisins, currants, dates, prunes, figs. Dried apricots are the best vegetable iron source and are a tangy addition. Mix in nuts: walnuts, cashews, peanuts, almonds. Mix in

seeds: sunflower seeds, toasted sesame seeds, poppy seeds. Your bread will be solid, compact, loaded with good food, and deliciously chewable.

Add herbs and spices: cinnamon, ginger, cardamon, caraway seeds, anise. If you sniff your dough, often you can tell what would taste good in it.

7. Mix in at least 5 cups of whole wheat flour. Then mix in new flours, any kind at all. Since unyeasted bread doesn't have to rise, gluten isn't such a critical factor as it is in yeasted bread. Rye flour, millet flour, soy flour, brown rice flour, buckwheat flour are all good. Roasted barley flour is especially nutty and sweet in unyeasted bread. So are sesame meal, peanut meal, cornmeal, you name it.

8. Keep mixing in flour with your spoon, then with your hand. *The amount of flour you add is the most variable quantity in unyeasted bread.* The quantity depends on how coarse-ground the flour is, and on what grain it comes from. Even different whole wheat flours vary in their ability to take up water. The amount of flour you add depends on what other solids you have mixed into your dough, on how liquid your liquid was, etc.. Never feel bound to use the exact amount of flour recommended in a recipe. Recipes are only approximations. Use your common sense.

9. When the dough holds together but is still slightly moist, lift it onto a floured counter, and knead to bind everything together. Keep spreading flour on the counter so the dough won't stick. Kneading is an intimate process between you and your bread. It is a spirit—calm and happy. And it cannot be rushed.

Unyeasted bread is moist and caky if you knead only a little flour into it. If you want a more bready bread, you have to add more flour and knead more. 300 kneads is a good number to aim for. You can feel when your dough stays together and is ready to be shaped.

10. Shape the dough into loaves which appeal to you. I like round balls—2 of them for 3 cups of liquid. I carve slashes or crosses on the top so air can get out and the crusts don't split during baking. Loaves should be baked on baking sheets lightly oiled or sprinkled with cornmeal or poppy seeds. For a really crunchy crust, cover a

rack in your oven with unglazed ceramic tiles, slide your loaves in, and bake them right on the tiles.

Occasionally you might shape your dough into lots of little balls, free-standing loaf-shaped loaves, or flat pancakes scored for easy breaking when hiking.

11. Your loaves can be baked right away. Or they can be left overnight, during which time some rising due to the yeast naturally present in the flour may occur. People talk about this rising reverently, but I have never had unyeasted breads rise during the night. One thing is true—flavors blend overnight. Overnight unyeasted bread is richer-tasting, has more body.

Bake the bread about 1 1/4 to 1 1/2 hours in a preheated 350 degrees F oven. Or start the bread from a cold oven and bake it for about 1 1/2 to 1 3/4 hours at 350 degrees F. Unyeasted bread is done when it's firm-crusted and a deep brown color. If you're in any doubt about a loaf's being done, leave it in the oven longer. Unyeasted breads are almost never overbaked, but it's very common to underbake them so the center is uncooked.

Unyeasted bread can be sliced easily if you have a good knife and a strong arm. It gets better every day. Don't wrap it—the crust will shelter the inside of a loaf while the flavors spread and mellow. The balls of sweetness around each raisin will grow larger every day; the nuttiness of walnuts will permeate the whole loaf; spicy flavors will work into every grain of flour.

Chewy Brown Rice Bread

The grainiest and most satisfying of breads—firm and close-packed, it's ideal for slicing thick or thin. Delicious spread with egg salad, cheese spreads, hummus.... In fact ideal for any open face sandwich. This is the best bread I make.

    3 cups hot water
    1/4 cup unrefined oil (Corn germ oil is best.)
    1 tablespoon sea salt
    4 cups cooked brown rice (1 1/2 cups uncooked)
    9 to 10 cups (more or less) whole wheat flour

1. In your bread bowl, mix together all the ingredients except the flour.
2. Gradually add the flour, stirring after each addition, until you can't stir any more. Then mix in more flour with your hand.
3. When the dough starts holding together, lift it onto a floured counter and start kneading. This is exercise! Add more flour to keep the dough from sticking to the counter. Knead 300 times, pausing to rest any time you want along the way. (My brother Eric makes unyeasted bread late at night. He lights a candle in the kitchen and pours a small glass of homemade wine. Then he kneads by candlelight, and after every 50 kneads he takes a sip.)
4. Shape the dough into 2 loaf-shaped loaves. The loaf shape is good so you can slice the bread for sandwiches, but any other shape works just as well.
5. Bake 1 1/4 to 1 1/2 hours at 350 degrees F. The loaves are done when they're browned and firm when you tap them.

Yield: 2 loaf-shaped loaves

Dense Pumpernickel

An unyeasted version of dark rye bread, with the exciting licorice taste of fennel. Good with all cheeses, especially Norwegian gjetost.

    3 cups potato water, coffee, or a mixture
    1/4 cup unrefined oil
    1/2 cup molasses
    1 tablespoon sea salt
    4 cups cooked rye berries (1 1/2 cups uncooked)
    2 tablespoons caraway seeds, ground
    2 tablespoons fennel seeds, ground
    5 cups whole wheat flour
    4 to 5 cups (more or less) rye flour

Grind the seeds in your grain mill or in a mortar and pestle.

Yield: 2 hefty loaves

I like using dense pumpernickel as the center of a long, lingering Scandinavian smør brød breakfast to share with friends. Dense pumpernickel is on the bread board with a bread knife. On another board I have cheeses: a Gouda or Edam, a creamy aged Brick cheese, and a block of brown gjetost. I use a cheese plane to shave off slices of the cheeses. On still another board or plate is a cucumber or two, a few green peppers sliced in rings, and some ripe tomatoes. There's a dish of unsalted butter and a pitcher of cream for coffee. Each person has a plate to collect these treasures on, and a good mug of steaming coffee. 'Spis, drikk, og vaer glad.' (Eat, drink, and be happy.)

Carob Date Bread

Carob satisfies your desire for a deep chocolatey taste without filling you with insatiable greed as does chocolate. It's also a good source of calcium. Carob bread tastes richer and richer as it gets older. When making the bread, you mix the carob powder with the oil and eggs first, so the oil will coat the carob particles and keep the loaf moist and tender. Roasted carob powder is the dark kind.

Carob bread is delicious with butter or cream cheese and honey. Or try this daring blend of tastes for lunch: carob date bread, Gorgonzola or Danish bleu cheese, and a big red apple.

 3 cups roasted carob powder
 1/4 cup unrefined oil
 2 or 3 large eggs
 3 cups milk or yoghurt
 1/4 cup honey
 1 tablespoon sea salt
 1/2 pound dates, whole or in big pieces
 10 cups (more or less) whole wheat flour

1. Mix the oil, carob powder, and eggs until they're creamy.
2. Add the milk gradually, mixing all the while to form a smooth paste.
3. Mix in everything else as in the general unyeasted bread recipe.
4. Knead, shape, and bake.

Variation:
—Add chopped walnuts.

Yield: 2 round loaves

Steve's Bread

The bread every lover of peanuts and dates dreams of.

     3 cups milk or yoghurt that didn't yoge
     1/4 cup unrefined oil (Peanut oil is best.)
     1/2 cup peanut butter
     1/4 cup honey
     1/4 cup molasses
     1 tablespoon sea salt
     1/2 pound peanuts, roasted in the oven
     1/2 pound dates, whole or in big pieces
     8 to 9 cups (more or less) whole wheat flour

Follow directions in the general unyeasted bread recipe.

Variation:
—Substitute 1/2 cup maple syrup for the honey and molasses.

Yield: 2 round loaves

Jenny's Poppy Seed Prune Bread

A gorgeous dark-gold loaf—textured with flecks of poppy and sunflower seeds, and with pieces of prune peeking out. It has little crunches in it, sweet spots, and a very subtle cinnamon and nutmeg dough. Good spread with nut butters, especially cashew butter.

- 3 cups hot water, vegetable water, or apple juice
- 1/4 cup unrefined oil
- 1/4 cup honey
- 2 tablespoons molasses
- 1 tablespoon sea salt
- 3 cups rolled oats, wheat flakes, rye flakes, or a combination
- 1 cup sunflower seeds, toasted in a pan
- 1/2 cup poppy seeds, toasted
- 4 handfuls prunes
- 1/2 teaspoon cinnamon
- 1/4 teaspoon nutmeg
- 8 to 9 cups (more or less) whole wheat flour

Follow directions in the general unyeasted bread recipe. If your prunes are hard, you might want to soak them overnight in water before you use them in bread.

Yield: 2 round loaves

Sweet Garbanzo Bread

Whole cooked garbanzos have the rich crunch of nuts. And with cardamon, raisins, and lemon, this bread is a perky nut and fruit cake. Good for breakfast and snacks.

3 cups hot water or water you cooked the garbanzos in
1/4 cup unrefined oil (Sesame oil is best.)
1/4 cup honey
1 tablespoon sea salt
2 to 3 cups cooked garbanzo beans (1 cup uncooked)
1 cup sesame seeds, toasted in a pan
Lots of raisins
Juice and grated rind of 1 lemon, orange, or lime
1 teaspoon ground cardamon
10 to 11 cups (more or less) whole wheat flour

Follow directions in the general unyeasted bread recipe.

Yield: 2 free-form, loaf-shaped loaves

Wings Of Life Bread

The bread this book is named for—strong, scrumptious, and inspiring, it's filled with ripe bananas, dried fruit, and walnuts. Try Wings Of Life any way, any time of the day.

2 1/2 cups yoghurt or yoghurt that didn't yoge
3 or 4 very ripe bananas
1/4 cup butter or sesame oil
1/4 cup honey
1 tablespoon sea salt
3 handfuls walnuts, in big pieces
3 handfuls dried apricots, in big pieces
3 handfuls raisins
9 to 10 cups (more or less) whole wheat flour

Follow directions in the general unyeasted bread recipe. To give your loaves a rich sheen, rub them lightly with butter when they're hot from the oven.

Variations:
—If you add more of the nuts or fruits than is called for, your bread will taste even better.
—Use part rye flour for a deeper taste.

Yield: 2 round loaves

Warning: This recipe should really be made with fresh ground whole wheat flour which is coarser and more aerated than store bought flour. If you must use store bought flour, be sure to knead the bread at least ten minutes. Please expect a very dense bread which is luscious and tasty; it in no way resembles breads made with yeast.

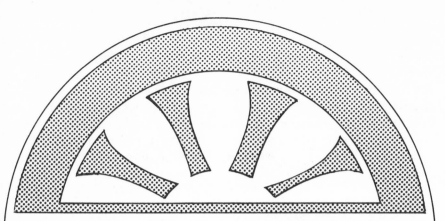

What To Put On Bread

A single thick slice of homemade bread, spread with butter, and piled high with grated cheese, avocado, tomato, cucumbers, and onions—that is what I call a sandwich. It's lush. You lose the effect entirely if you try to close the sandwich with a second slice of bread. You can't see what you're eating, you can't appreciate the colors and textures, and you can't pile your bread so high. Moreover, if you try to slice homemade bread thin, as you have to for closed sandwiches, it falls apart. Respect your bread.

YOU CAN'T BEAT CHEESE

Legend has it that cheese was invented in prehistoric times when a travelling trader from Arabia stopped to eat his lunch while crossing a mountainous section of Asia. He raised up his canteen, made from a partially dried sheep stomach, to take a swig of fresh milk. When he got only a trickle instead, he cut open the skin to see what had happened. Lo and behold, the rennet in the sheep's stomach has curdled his fresh milk to a solid mass with only a little liquid around it. Cheesemaking spread from there until today almost every region of the world has its own special kind of cheese.

Whenever possible I try to buy cheeses made with vegetable enzymes rather than with rennet, since the rennet enzyme comes from the linings of young calves' stomachs, and the calves are killed to obtain it. A few years ago it was almost impossible to buy rennetless cheeses, and ricotta was the only cheese made without rennet. Now, however, more good cottage cheeses and hard cheeses coagulated without rennet are available, and if we encourage cheesemakers by buying rennetless cheeses, we'll have a wider selection all the time.

Processed cheeses are an abomination. Besides tasting insipid, they're made by grinding up real cheese, heating it with salt, adding emulsifiers to keep it from separating, and often coloring it artificially.

Cheese should always be eaten at room temperature. You miss a good deal of the flavor and the smooth texture of a cheese if you eat it cold.

Cheddar cheese is good grated for sandwiches. Cheeses from Scandinavia, Switzerland, and the Netherlands are particularly good eaten in the thin slices you get with an ost hyvel, a Scandinavian cheese plane. Several thin slices from a plane are perfect for eating on buttered bread. Try arranging lettuce, cucumber and green pepper slices, sliced radishes, onion rings, and a lacy tangle of alfalfa sprouts on cheese sandwiches for a smør brød—a Scandinavian open face sandwich board. Says my Norwegian Grandma Magna, 'You can put anything you like on an open face sandwich. Anything.'

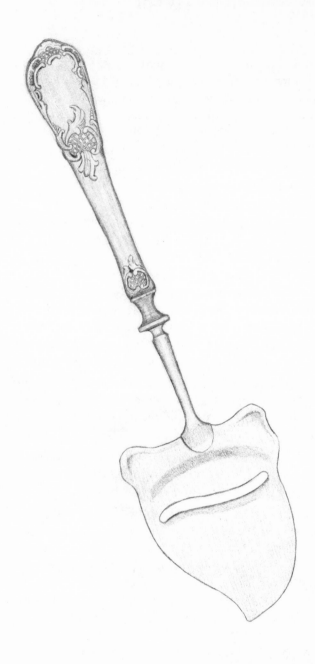

OST HYVEL—A Scandinavian cheese plane for cutting cheese in thin slices

Hot Cheese Sandwiches

There's nothing quite as scrumptious as a hot cheese sandwich, especially when it's cold outside. To make them, I start by toasting thick slices of an herbed grainy bread. Then I butter the untoasted side and cover it with any of the variations below, then pop it under the broiler to heat it throughout and to melt the cheese.

Sauerkraut and Swiss cheese (Good on rye bread)

Bavarian mustard and Swiss cheese

Melted bleu cheese with chopped almonds, returned to the broiler until the almonds are lightly toasted

Apple rings sautéed in butter and Cheddar cheese

Cream cheese, sliced tomato, Swiss cheese, and a sprinkling of dried basil, oregano, and thyme

Little pizzas—Homemade tomato sauce, mozzarella and Parmesan cheeses, heated under the broiler or in the oven until the cheeses are bubbly

Melted cheese & salad sandwich—Butter a crusty roll, cover with mild Cheddar or Monterey jack cheese, and heat until just bubbly. Arrange lettuce on top. Pour heated herb and garlic vinaigrette dressing over everything.

Cheddar & Homemade Pickle Spread

The kind of spread you'd expect a farm grandmother to serve you. If it's made up in advance and aged in the refrigerator, it will taste even better as the flavors blend.

  1/2 pound Cheddar cheese, grated (2 cups)
  1/2 cup finely minced homemade pickles, or pimentos, or a
    mixture
  Homemade mayonnaise

1. Mix the cheese and pickles.
2. Add just enough mayonnaise to moisten the mixture to spreading consistency.

Yield: 2 cups

Cheddar & Wine Spread

A smooth but pungent spread, with the mellow purple color of red wine.

  1/2 pound Cheddar cheese, grated (2 cups)
  1/4 cup red wine
  1/4 cup ricotta cheese
  2 cloves garlic, mashed

Beat all the ingredients together with a fork until smooth. If possible, age it for about a day or 2 before serving.

Yield: 2 cups

Cream Cheese Spreads

To be appreciated fully, cream cheese spreads must be as thick as the slice of bread you put them on.

Cream cheese mixed with lots of chopped black olives

Cream cheese mixed with coarsely chopped walnuts

Cream cheese mixed with a little chopped crystallized ginger

Blue Cheese Spread

Of the bleu cheeses available, I particularly recommend Danish bleu or Italian Gorgonzola, which is very soft and creamy. Top sandwiches with ripe tomato slices and chopped chives.

  Bleu cheese, crumbled
  Cottage cheese
  Fresh chives or parsley, finely chopped
  Freshly ground black pepper
  Yoghurt

Mix in just enough yoghurt to make the mixture spreadable.

Cheese Fondue

Cheese fondue is a melty cheese and wine sauce which you serve hot at the table. Everyone dips bread cubes into it. There is a lot of rigamarole about the proper cheeses and the proper wines for fondue, but I disregard it. Although I don't have direct evidence, I am sure fondue was invented in Switzerland to use up bits of old bread, scraps of cheese, and the ends of bottles of wine. Some of my best fondues have been made from Cheddar cheese and red wine, and had cubes of pumpernickel dipped in them. You don't even need a fondue pot for cheese fondue. You can make it in the top of a double boiler, then keep it hot on the table by resting it in the bottom full of water you've just boiled. If you don't have a double boiler, you can make fondue in a saucepan, and rest that pan in a larger pan full of boiling water.

Serve cheese fondue with salad for an intimate dinner, or serve it alone for a late night party. I don't know where the custom started, but fondue is almost always served on New Year's Eve.

1 pound cheese, or combination of cheeses, grated
3 tablespoons whole wheat flour
Freshly ground black pepper
Nutmeg
1 or 2 cloves garlic
2 cups wine

1. In a large bowl, mix the grated cheese, flour, pepper, and nutmeg.
2. Mash the garlic into your fondue pot or saucepan. Add the wine, and heat it on top of the stove until it just starts to bubble.
3. Gradually stir in the cheese mixture. Continue heating and stirring until all the cheese melts. If the mixture is too thick, add some more wine. If it's too thin, grate a little more cheese, mix it with more flour, and stir it in. The flour is the thickener.
4. Taste. You might want to add more nutmeg or a little more pepper.
5. Carry the fondue to the table and keep it warm with a flame or with boiling water.
6. People sharing the fondue spear little bread cubes you've cut from bread you've just made or bread starting to dry out. Besides

bread cubes, cubes of apple, raw cauliflower, carrots, or celery are good dipped in cheese fondue.

Variations:

—Add a squeeze of fresh lemon juice or a dash of kirsch to the cooked fondue.

—Herbs, such as caraway seeds or basil, added right at the beginning, give you a more savory fondue.

Yield: Serves 4

BUTTER

Butter is one of the older man-made foods. A mythical nomad carrying creamy milk around with him jiggled it so much that when he opened his flask, a big lump of butter floated up. Butter today can be made from unsoured (sweet) cream or from specially soured (ripened) cream. Salt is an optional ingredient. I think Danish-style ripened cream butters are the best, but they're very hard to get. After them I prefer an unsalted sweet cream butter. Good butter is really good, and if you're making your own bread, it's worth sampling around until you find a butter which pleases you.

Homemade Sweet Cream Butter

Here's how to make a small amount. With a churn, you can make large quantities of butter following approximately the same procedure.

Heavy cream or top milk
Pinch salt, if you want salted butter

1. Put the cream and salt, if you're using it, in a jar with a tight-fitting lid. Close it.
2. Shake and shake. The tiny butterfat globules in the cream will combine and start to settle out.
3. After 10 to 15 minutes of shaking, a spongy mass of butterfat will start to form. The liquid is the buttermilk—water, milk protein, milk sugar, and salts.
4. Shake more. The spongy mass will collapse into a solid lump.
5. Continue shaking until the lump looks like butter. Then pour off the buttermilk and cool the butter. The buttermilk is still quite rich. Try using it in your next batch of bread.

Garlic Butter

Plant cloves of garlic in a garden or a flowerpot, and they will send up green shoots. You can dig up these 'garlic scallions', chop them, cloves and shoot, then mix them into soft butter to make garlic butter. Or you can mash whole cloves of garlic.

The best way I've found to mash garlic is to have a special garlic mortar and pestle. I put peeled cloves of garlic in the mortar with a little salt to absorb the garlic juice, then smash the cloves with the pestle. The garlic-salt comes out easily. And I don't have to wash the mortar and pestle for anything else. If you don't have a mortar and pestle you wish to sacrifice to garlic, you can mash the garlic with salt on a cutting board using a dull-edged table knife.

Mix garlic butter with a little freshly grated Parmesan cheese and chopped fresh parsley, spread it on slices of bread, and reheat the bread in the oven. It's a zippier version of that wonderful hot garlic bread you eat with Italian meals, or with omelettes and salads.

Fresh Herb Butters

This herb butter will taste strongly of garlic when you make it. However, if you age it in the refrigerator, each fresh herb taste will come forward.

    1/4 pound butter (1/2 cup)
    1/4 cup minced fresh parsley
    1 tablespoon minced fresh chives
    1 tablespoon minced fresh dill
    1 small clove garlic, mashed
    Squirt fresh lemon juice

Leave the butter out at room temperature until it's soft, then whip together all the ingredients with a fork.

Variations:
—Add fresh basil, marjoram, scallions, or finely minced shallots.

Yield: 1 scant cupful

EGGS

Slices of hard-cooked egg with lettuce on homemade bread spread with homemade mayonnaise or herb butter is simple and delicious.

Boil enough water to cover the eggs. Put the eggs in, then cover the pot and simmer the eggs for 12 minutes. Try to keep the water just under boiling so the eggs will end up with tender yellow yolks. After 12 minutes, plop the eggs into cold water right away and they'll be easy to peel.

A good way to peel a hard-cooked egg is to roll it around on a counter, cracking the egg shell in a mosaic all over the egg so the shell is held together only by the membrane underneath. Try to pull on the membrane, and everything will peel off easily. If you find an egg in the refrigerator, and aren't sure whether you've hard-cooked it or not, put it on its side on a table and spin it around. A hard-cooked egg will keep spinning, while an uncooked egg will slow down and stop spinning very quickly because of the inertia of the liquid in it.

Egg Salad With Almonds

The almonds add a chew and a delicious new flavor to traditional egg salad. Mound egg salad on a slice of buttered homemade bread (Chewy brown rice bread is ideal.), then top the sandwich with cucumber and tomato slices, and alfalfa sprouts. Or serve egg salad in a cup of lettuce as part of a salad plate.

    2 hard-cooked eggs
    10 almonds, chopped in chunks
    1/2 medium onion, finely chopped
    Homemade mayonnaise
    Fresh parsley, finely chopped
    Sea salt

1. Peel the eggs, and cut them into fine pieces in a bowl. The most efficient method is to use 2 knives. You hold 1 knife in each hand, and slice them across each other in opposite directions.
2. Mix in the almonds and onion.
3. Stir in a little homemade mayonnaise. Add only enough to moisten the salad. You don't want egg salad to be soupy.
4. Add salt and taste. The right amount of salt is crucial in egg salad.
5. Mix in fresh parsley.

Variations:
—Mix in some cottage cheese to lighten and extend the egg. (A good-tasting nutritious cheat)
—Add chopped fresh tomatoes or chopped green peppers. Add finely minced scallions, chives, or other fresh green herbs. Always taste for salt.

Yield: Serves 2

VEGETABLES

Open face salad sandwiches are especially good on savory bread, and on dark rye breads like pumpernickel. I would start by spreading the bread with thick homemade mayonnaise, garlic mayonnaise, or fresh herb butter. After that, what you put on them is really up to you. Avocado slices are sublime. And marinated mushrooms are juicy served on the side of a salad sandwich plate.

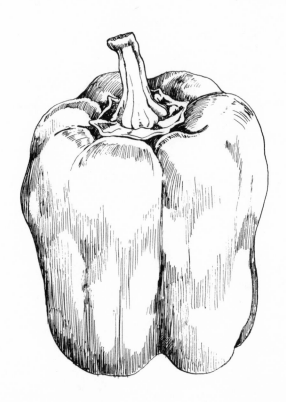

Hot Vegetable Sandwiches

My mother taught me to make a delicious sandwich with sliced green peppers and onions. Sauté them until limp in olive oil. (Olive oil is crucial here for flavor.) Slice wheat soy French bread in half the long way, or slice any crusty homemade rolls in half. Toast the bread or rolls under the broiler, then butter them. Cover the buttered bread thickly with the hot cooked onions and peppers.

Another hot vegetable sandwich is made by piling buttered French bread with mounds of mushrooms sautéed in butter with a little sherry and rosemary.

Creamed Broccoli On Toast

Served with a salad, hot creamed broccoli sandwiches are the
perfect lunch on a cold day.

    2 onions, sliced
    2 large stalks broccoli, cut in fairly large pieces
    2 cups whole wheat white sauce, with nutmeg and 1 cup grated
        Cheddar cheese added (See Index)

1. Stir-fry the onions in butter until they're limp. Add the broccoli
and keep stir-frying until it's tender.
2. Meanwhile make the sauce. Make basic whole wheat white sauce
with nutmeg, then remove the pan from the heat and stir in the
Cheddar cheese.
3. Stir the sauce into the broccoli and onions, and continue
heating until it's warm.
4. Spoon the sauce over toasted, buttered homemade bread.

Variations:
—Add tarragon or sherry to the white sauce.
—Try mushrooms or asparagus instead of broccoli.

Yield: Serves 4

Guacamole

Guacamole is an avocado spread with that 'close to Mexico' zing. Most simply, it's avocados mashed with plenty of salt. From there you can add garlic, tomato, onions, spices, and sour cream. The sour cream adds smoothness to the dip. The secret of my guacamole is ground cumin.

I generally buy avocados unripe, then ripen them at home so I can catch them at the peak of their flavor. An unripe avocado is hard, but as it ripens it gets softer until when it's ready it will be soft enough to keep the imprint of your fingers when you squeeze it lightly. To hasten ripening, store an avocado in a bowlful of flour. To peel an avocado, cut it in half the long way and take out the pit. Slice each half into about four slices lengthwise, then peel each piece.

To make a guacamole salad sandwich, lightly butter a slice of bread and spread guacamole thick on it. Lay tomato slices over that and snip scallions over everything. You can also use guacamole as a dip for carrot sticks, celery or green pepper sticks, raw cauliflowerettes or cucumber spears. I like guacamole dips before Mexican meals.

Always make guacamole fresh, as it will discolor and change flavor on standing.

    1 ripe avocado
    1/4 small onion or 2 scallions, finely chopped
    1 tablespoon sour cream
    Squirt fresh lime or lemon juice
    1/2 teaspoon ground cumin
    1 or 2 cloves garlic, mashed
    1/2 teaspoon sea salt
    1/4 medium tomato, finely chopped (optional)

    1. With a fork or potato masher, mash the avocado pulp together with all the other ingredients. Beat with a fork until it's fluffy and smooth.
    2. Taste. Add more salt if it needs it, more cumin for more bite, or more sour cream for a smoother spread.

Yield: Serves 2 or 3

NUT & SEED BUTTERS

Peanut Butter

Peanut butter is a delicious and nutritious food. The peanut—not actually a nut, but a legume (related to beans like kidney beans and soybeans)—is a good source of protein and an excellent source of B vitamins and minerals. Natural peanut butters are simply whole peanuts roasted then ground up with some salt often added for flavor. I especially like buying peanut butter from stores where you can grind it fresh or can fill your own jar from big tubs. Both ways it has a fresher taste than peanut butter from little jars. Natural peanut butters will separate on standing, since some of the peanut oil will rise to the surface. You can simply mix the oil back in when you use the peanut butter, or you can leave the peanut butter jar upside-down, then turn it right-side up when you want to use it.

I strongly recommend buying peanut butters from natural foods stores rather than buying commercial peanut butters. Commercial peanut butters are made from blanched peanuts—peanuts with the reddish skins, which contain part of the nutrients, removed. They have sugar added, and quite often large amounts of salt. Finally, in commercial peanut butters the natural unsaturated oils of the peanut are saturated to give you the plastic non-separating spreadability so touted by advertisements. (Saturated fats are solid at room temperature rather than liquid as are the natural unsaturated oils in the peanut.) Not only does artificial saturation remove the fresh taste of the peanut and waste energy, but saturated fats have been implicated in atherosclerosis.

Tahini & Sesame Butter

Tahini is a thin butter made by grinding hulled sesame seeds. It velvetizes everything it's mixed into, and adds a subtle sweet flavor. If you whip it with lemon juice, it becomes light and fluffy like mayonnaise. Whipped tahini mixed with grated cheese, chopped lettuce, and chopped tomatoes is a delicious stuffing for pockets of Arabic bread. And whipped tahini is the basis for the Middle Eastern spreads hummus and baba ganoush. Tahini is a good staple to keep in your kitchen—you'll use it a lot.

Sesame butter is made by grinding whole sesame seeds. It's better for you than tahini, since most of the minerals, especially calcium, of the sesame seed are in the hull. It lacks the velvet touch and doesn't whip up. However, sesame butter has a dark rich color and taste comparable to that of peanut butter, and it's delicious spread on homemade bread and used everywhere you'd use peanut butter.

Homemade Nut & Seed Butters

If you have a hand grain mill, nut and seed butters are surprisingly easy to make. Like everything homemade, they taste fresher and better than anything you could buy. Toasted butters are stronger-tasting than untoasted butters.

Untoasted butters
Cashew butter, sesame butter, almond butter

1. Grind the nuts or seeds once through your grain mill on a fine grind. You'll get a nut or seed meal.
2. Mix the meal with enough unrefined oil to make a creamy, spreadable paste. Whenever possible, use the oil from the nut or seed you've ground. (For instance, use sesame oil to make sesame butter.) If you can't match oils, corn germ oil is versatile, and is especially good for mixing with ground cashews to make cashew butter. For variety I often use dairy butter to cream nut butters. It makes more of a nut pâté.
3. Add salt to taste.

Toasted butters
Peanut butter, toasted sesame butter, toasted sunflower butter

1. Roast the nuts or seeds in the oven before you grind them. I usually bake them while I'm baking bread. Bake them in flat pans until they're a light brown, stirring every now and then. You can experiment with roasting times to get the flavors you like.
2. Proceed as for untoasted butters.

Nut & Seed Butter Sandwich Ideas

The juiciness of fruits and vegetables goes perfectly with sticky nut butters.

Peanut butter and sliced cucumbers

Peanut butter and sliced ripe tomatoes

Peanut butter mixed with finely chopped onion, garnished with carrot sticks

Peanut butter and sliced bananas

Peanut butter and dates, garnished with orange slices

Toasted sesame butter used in all the ways you'd use peanut butter

Cashew butter and honey, sprinkled with sunflower seeds

Peanut Butter & Yoghurt Spread

This is good stuff, with just the right amount of peanut butter and just the right amount of sweetness. I'm addicted to this spread for breakfast and for late night snacks.

> 2 parts yoghurt
> 1 part peanut butter
> Raisins
> Honey or maple syrup

Mix everything together, adding honey or maple syrup to taste. If you make the spread the day before you want to use it, the raisins will soak up liquid and the spread will be much firmer.

Variations:
—Use toasted sesame butter instead of peanut butter.
—Use homemade buttermilk instead of yoghurt.

Ground Almond Spread

Delicious on crackers.

> Whole almonds, roasted and ground up in your grain mill
> Onion or scallions, finely minced
> Dash tamari sauce
> Homemade mayonnaise

1. Mix the ground almonds, onion, and tamari sauce.
2. Add mayonnaise to moisten the mixture to spreading consistency.

Baba Ganoush

A Middle Eastern spread made from mashed roasted eggplant, tahini, garlic, and lemon juice. As with hummus, the key to a good texture is whipping up the tahini with lemon juice before adding it to the eggplant.

Use baba ganoush on sandwiches, to fill pockets of Arabic bread, or as a dip for wedges of Arabic bread and fresh vegetable sticks.

> 1 medium eggplant
> 4 or 5 cloves garlic, mashed
> 1 teaspoon sea salt
> 1/2 cup tahini
> Juice 1 lemon
> 1/2 cup finely minced fresh parsley
> Sprinkle cayenne pepper

1. Prick the whole unpeeled eggplant in a few places with a fork. Then roast it until it's soft throughout and collapsed. Either roast it on hot coals, turning it once so it roasts evenly. Or stick it with a long-handled fork and hold it in the open flame of a gas burner, turning it until it's soft and the skin is charred and cracked all around. This takes about 15 minutes. Or place the eggplant on a baking sheet and broil it about 4 inches from the heat in an electric oven. Turn it to cook all sides, and continue until the eggplant is completely collapsed. This takes about 20 minutes.
2. When the eggplant is cool enough to handle, peel off the charred skin.
3. Cut the eggplant in half lengthwise, and chop it finely. Beat the pulp with a fork until it's smooth.
4. In a separate bowl mix the garlic and salt. Stir in the tahini. With a wooden spoon, beat in the lemon juice.
5. Beat the tahini mixture into the mashed eggplant a little at a time. The mixture should whip up nicely and turn a lighter color.
6. Add the fresh parsley and cayenne pepper. Taste.

Variations:
—Use sesame butter instead of tahini.
—Baba gazook—Use a medium-size zucchini instead of the eggplant. It has a lighter taste.

Yield: 2 cups

Hummus

A Middle Eastern spread made from mashed chick peas, tahini, garlic, and lemon juice. I think it's one of the world's great foods, and I feel perfectly content after eating it. The key to a smooth creamy texture is whipping up the tahini with lemon juice and water in a separate bowl.

Top hummus sandwiches with tomato or cucumber slices, or with grated Cheddar cheese. Use hummus to fill pockets of Arabic bread. Or use hummus as a dip for wedges of Arabic bread, cucumber sticks, carrot sticks, and green pepper sticks.

> 2 cups cooked chick peas (1 cup uncooked)
> 4 or 5 cloves garlic, mashed
> 1 teaspoon sea salt
> 1/2 cup tahini
> Juice 1 lemon
> 2 to 6 tablespoons (more or less) chick pea cooking liquid
>   or water
> 1/2 cup finely chopped fresh parsley

1. Mash the cooked chick peas with a fork, grind them through a meat grinder, or grind them through your grain mill.
2. Mix the garlic and salt in a separate bowl. Stir in the tahini. With a wooden spoon, beat in the lemon juice. Add a little cooking liquid or water and beat some more. Continue adding liquid and beating until the sauce has the consistency of thick mayonnaise and holds its shape almost solidly in a spoon.
3. Beat the tahini mixture from step 2 into the mashed chick peas. Add a little at a time, and continue beating until it's smooth. Add some more. At the end, if the mixture is too thick, beat in a little more liquid until it's spreadable.
4. Mix in the fresh parsley and taste. You might want to add a little more salt.

Variation:
—Use sesame butter instead of tahini. The hummus will be denser, but will have a delicious flavor.

Yield: 2 cups

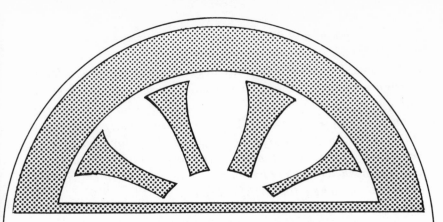

Cooked Grains & Beans

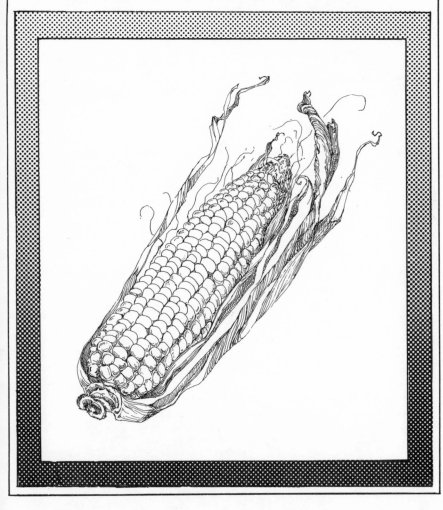

I use certain grains and beans frequently and always try to have them on hand. I especially recommend brown rice and millet as staple grains. For a first adventure in bean cookery I suggest lentils. Lentils are readily available, even in commercial grocery stores, they cook quickly, and they can be used in a variety of dishes. After that, if you give in to temptation as I do, you'll find yourself buying quite a collection of grains and beans. They keep for a long time (years), so you can buy as many as you want and line them up in glass jars on shelves. It's convenient to have an assortment ready to use, and they make a fine artistic display.

Grains

Whole grains are good sources of protein, B vitamins, minerals, and fiber. When grains are refined, many nutrients are lost. For example, brown rice is a much better source of the whole complex of B vitamins and trace minerals than white rice or enriched white rice (to which only a few nutrients are added back). Brown rice also has the fiber of its outer layer, whereas this is missing from white rice.

Brown rice

Rice is the most important single staple food in the world, and is eaten by more than half the human race. I like short-grain brown rice best. It's the sweetest. It's also beautiful: each seed is a little oval with a pale green streak. Rice is good for eating with vegetable stir-fries, in soups, in breads, casseroles, and for breakfast.

Millet

Millet is one of the most ancient of cultivated grains, but I feel as if I discovered it. It's light, fluffy, and nutty-tasting. Millet cooks quickly, and can be used anywhere rice is used. I especially like it with vegetable stir-fries, and for one of my favorite dinner dishes—millet soufflé.

Whole wheat

The same wheat berries you grind for flour are delicious cooked up whole. They always stay chewier than brown rice, so they're good for texture. A three-grain mixture of brown rice, millet, and wheat berries (each cooked up separately then mixed together) is my favorite for eating with stir-fried vegetables.

Cracked wheat is coarse-ground wheat berries. I make it by grinding wheat berries once through my grain mill on a coarse grind. Cooked in water with dates and a pinch of salt, it's a delicious breakfast cereal.

Wheat flakes are wheat berries which have been steam-cooked, then rolled out. Flakes cook up very quickly, and can be used anywhere you'd use wheat berries, although they're not as firm. Use them in granola.

Bulghur is wheat berries which have been pre-cooked, cracked into smaller pieces, then dried out. To make bulghur from wheat berries, cook the berries (See instructions this chapter). Spread them on a baking tray and dry them in the oven while you're baking bread or a casserole. When they're dry, grind them on a very coarse grind through your grain mill. That's bulghur. It only has to be soaked to be eaten. (See tabbouleh for a bulghur salad.)

Pasta is the Italian way to use wheat. Recipes for homemade pasta are at the end of this chapter.

Rye
Rye berries are similar to wheat berries, but with a stronger flavor. When I'm cooking from foreign cookbooks, I use cooked rye berries in place of the meat in recipes, especially in place of lamb.

Rye flakes are to rye berries what wheat flakes are to wheat berries. Use them in granola too.

Barley
Barley is the oldest cultivated grain in man's history. Since the outer coat of barley seeds is tough, the barley you buy today is usually 'pearled'. Pearling removes the outer layers of the seed, so pearled barley has some nutrients missing. But the barley in natural foods stores is pearled less than commercial barley, leaving it slightly darker and more nutritious. Barley has a unique chewy texture and a delicious flavor—perfect in casseroles and soups. A little roasted barley flour is a sweet treat in bread.

Oats
Oats are so delicious and sweet, it's hard to believe they're just a plain grain. We mostly eat oat flakes (rolled oats) in granola, oatmeal bread, or cooked up as a breakfast cereal. Cook rolled oats in two volumes of water with a pinch of salt for breakfast. Good additions are raisins, dates, sliced bananas, or sliced almonds.

Steel-cut oats are widely available in natural foods stores and are good to cook up for breakfast or to use in bread.

Buckwheat
The most flavorful grain. Whole buckwheat kernels, called buckwheat groats or kasha, are good cooked up as a breakfast cereal or as a grainy side dish for stir-fried vegetables. My friends tell me there is only one way to cook kasha: mix one cup of kasha with a well-beaten egg, toss them together in a hot, lightly oiled saucepan until the egg is cooked, then add half a teaspoon of salt and one and one-half cups of water. Bring the water to a boil, cover the pot, and

simmer ten to twelve minutes. Kasha cooked this way is flavorful and fluffy.

Buckwheat flour makes the lightest, most delicate crêpes.

Corn

Corn has always been the backbone food of our country. It was grown here by the Indians long before white men arrived; and corn kept our early European settlers alive. I grew up in a corn area, and remember as a little girl running through rows of corn much higher than my head. I've always loved fresh corn-on-the-cob. Now, just recently, I've started to cook with dried corn ground into cornmeal. I like the honest taste of cornmeal mush for breakfast (cornmeal cooked in boiling water with a pinch of salt). I like cornbread with soups, cornmeal crusts in tamale pie. I'm developing a passion for corn tortillas, stuffed with beans, onions, cheese, avocados....

You can buy cornmeal in natural foods stores. Or buy whole dried corn and grind it in your grain mill.

Beans

Most beans have the same general nutritive properties: they're excellent sources of B vitamins, minerals, fiber, and protein. I keep thinking I have a favorite bean; then someone will cook me a new one—black-eyed peas, white marrow beans.... Each bean is delicious in a different way.

Lentils

Lentils are quick to cook and versatile. I use them in casseroles, in dense salads with fresh dill, and especially in my soups. Lentil soups have been around for a long time: in the *Bible* Esau sold his birthright to his brother Jacob for 'bread and pottage of lentils'. (Genesis XXV: 29-34)

Soybeans

Soybeans seem to be the popular bean nowadays, since they have a very high protein content and also a lot of oil which gives them richness. (Soybeans may be up to twenty per cent oil, whereas other beans are about one to five per cent oil.) Soybeans can be cooked up and mixed in soups or casseroles.

In China, soybeans are made into a lot of special foods. The soybean products we find most commonly in this country are soy sauce (or tamari sauce) and soybean curd, called tofu. In Chinese stores you can also get dried soybean skins, dried smoked bean curd, and soy cheese. They're all good mixed in vegetable stir-fries.

Soy flakes are steamed, rolled-out soybeans. They cook much more quickly than soybeans, so they can be made up at the last minute.

Green soybeans are soybeans harvested before they dry on the vines. They're delicious, with a greener, fresher taste than the regular golden soybeans.

Kidney beans
Kidney beans are grown near where I live, so they're undoubtedly my favorites. This isn't just regional prejudice: local beans seem to be more tender and succulent when they're cooked up. Kidney beans are good in soups, in cashew chili, and in all Mexican cooking.

Pinto beans
These are very similar to kidney beans, only they're speckled like little horses. They're the real Mexican bean. I cook them up and make them into cashew chili, into fillings for enchiladas, or serve them as a side dish for Mexican meals, mixed with chopped onion and grated cheese.

Garbanzo beans (chick peas)
The more I eat chick peas, the more I like them. They're the bean for minestrone soup, for marinating and tossing in salads, for mashing up for hummus. Chick peas have a soft, firm texture to bite into, and a very mild but gorgeously beany flavor. Chick peas are the perfect introduction for people who aren't used to eating beans.

Black beans
These have the deepest, darkest flavor of all. Black bean soup is a Cuban specialty. I helped judge a 'Great Bean Bake-off' last year, and a Cuban woman's black bean soup was the tastiest dish there.

Peanuts
Peanuts are actually beans, not nuts. They can be cooked up for soups, and have a rich taste which bears no resemblance to peanut butter or roasted peanuts.

General Considerations

Aside from general guidelines, I specify no rigid cooking times and exact amounts of water for cooking grains and beans. Each kind of grain or bean, even each variety of the same kind, cooks up a little differently. My mother worked on a project trying to discover the perfect method for cooking rice when she was in college. She found that rice varies so much the best method was to watch the rice cook. That's almost my method in a nutshell: watch what you're doing. Taste what you're cooking to see if it's done and tender; and add more water as it's needed.

I like to have grains and beans already cooked on hand ready to be used in soups, breads, casseroles, or salads. Stored in a jar in the refrigerator, a cooked grain or bean will keep for at least one week.

High altitudes
At high altitudes, because of the lower air pressure, water boils at a lower temperature and therefore can never get hot enough to cook grains and beans quickly. If you live at an elevation significantly above sea level, plan on longer cooking—up to twice the approximate times I specify— except in a pressure cooker.

Amount of water
Some grains, like millet, should be cooked in a little water for a short time, so they're still crunchy. With others, it's no disaster if you add too much water. Beans taste best when cooked in plenty of water so you have a thick broth at the end. Never throw away cooking water. Extra grain and bean waters are excellent added to soups, or are good bread liquids.

Soaking
Soaking grains and beans before you cook them is a good idea. Soak them overnight if you plan ahead. Soaked grains and beans take less time to cook. And since soaking starts swelling them gradually, they keep their shape and texture much better on cooking.

Toasting
Grains will pick up an extra nutty flavor if they're pan-toasted before they're cooked or soaked. Shake the dry grains around in a dry pan until they start to brown. Or shake them in an oiled or buttered pan for an extra-rich taste.

Cooked Grains & Beans/85

Baking

Whenever I bake bread or a casserole, I like to fill up the oven with pans of grains or beans. Baked grains and beans have a clean, separate texture. And when you bake them, you can add herbs, spices, nuts, raisins, and onions or other seasonings for a rich blend of flavors—pilaf style. (I would not bake grains or beans unless using the oven already. It uses too much power.)

If I can, I soak the grains or beans overnight before I cook them. If not, I start soaking them the minute I think of it.

1. Put the grains or beans and the water they've been soaking in into a baking pan or a casserole dish with a cover. Add extra water or vegetable water until the water comes up to the first joint of your your thumb when you rest its tip on top of the grain or bean layer. (This is a good guide for all kinds of grain and bean cookery.) Try to choose a pan big enough so this fills only half of it. Otherwise what you're cooking will boil over in the oven.

2. Add a drip of oil so the grains won't stick and a dash of salt for flavor. Mix in seasonings if you'd like; dice in a few onions or some celery; then perhaps add a dash of sherry or tamari sauce for grains. (Two special hints: use thyme for brown rice and coriander for lentils.)

3. Stir up the mixture, then cover the pan and put it into the oven along with the bread or casserole you're baking.

4. When the bread or casserole is done, turn off the oven and leave the grains or beans in. They'll continue cooking as the oven cools down. Leave them in the oven for a total of about 2 to 2 1/2 hours. (Brown rice, millet, and lentils will be done earlier.) After 2 1/2 hours, I've found all soaked grains and beans will be done, or very close to done. If anything isn't cooked completely, just finish it on top of the stove.

Stove-Top Simmering

All grains and beans can be cooked on top of the stove. And since you can watch them, it's easiest to monitor how well they're getting done, and to taste them for tenderness. Beans simmered on top of the stove in an earthenware pot have a rich deep flavor you can't duplicate by any other method of cooking.

1. Put the grains or beans in a big pot with a lid. Cover them with water, and for grains pour in more water until it reaches your first thumb joint when you touch your thumb to the top of the grains. For beans add extra water. Don't plan on cooking to dryness. Add a bit of oil so the grains or beans don't clump together, and add a dash of salt for flavor.

2. Cover the pot, bring the water to a boil, and then lower the heat so the water is just simmering. Don't stir and the grains will stay separated.

3. As the cooking progresses, add more water as it's needed. Keep testing for tenderness, either by sticking a fork in beans or by biting a grain. Beans and grains are done when they're tender. It's very casual, and completely to your liking. (A chart of approximate stove-top simmering times for soaked grains and beans follows.)

Special considerations:
—I like to cook brown rice, millet, and lentils to dryness to keep their fragile texture. This requires more attention. After 20 minutes for lentils, 35 minutes for rice, or 20 minutes for millet, lift off the pot lid and check what's going on. If you like the grains or beans the way they are, kind of chewy, take the lid off the pot and stir with chopsticks until all the water has evaporated. (Chopsticks keep the grains from glopping together.) If you want the grains or beans more well-done, add a little more water, stir it, and cover the pot again. The more water you give the grains or beans, the softer they will be. You're in control. Just take the lid off the pot whenever you feel your grains are ready, and stir them around for a few minutes to dry them.

Pressure Cooking

If you want to eat grains or beans and don't have any cooked up, pressure cooking is definitely the fastest method. Grains which would take four hours on top of the stove are done in twenty to twenty-five minutes. And pressure-cooked grains or beans don't have to be pre-soaked. In general, when deciding on how long to cook a particular grain or bean in the pressure cooker, I'd rather slightly undercook it than boil it to a mush. Anything undercooked can be simmered a little longer on top of the stove; but if it's overdone, it's past repair.

If you're planning on buying a pressure cooker, I recommend getting a big one. Mine is six quarts. With a big cooker, you can cook fairly large quantities of grains or beans, and still leave them plenty of head space to foam.

1. Pour the beans or grains you're going to cook into the pressure cooker.
2. Cover them with water, and add enough more so that if you touch your thumb on top of the beans or grains, the water reaches up to your first thumb joint. Extra water is best here: you don't want anything to dry up in the pressure cooker.
3. Pour in about 1 tablespoon of unrefined oil to prevent foaming and a pinch of salt for flavor.
4. Cover the cooker. Bring it slowly up to 15 pounds pressure. When the pressure gauge starts jiggling or rocking, start measuring your cooking time. (A chart of approximate pressure cooking times for unsoaked grains and beans follows.)
5. Cook. Adjust the heat so there is a comfortable jiggle of the gauge about once a minute, or so the gauges of the rocking type rock gently.
6. At the end of the cooking time, bring down the pressure, and open the cooker.

Variation:
—About 5 minutes before the end of each cooking time given in the chart, turn off the heat under the pressure cooker. The heat left in the burner plus the built-up pressure in the cooker will finish cooking the grains or beans in about 20 minutes rather than the 5 minutes it would take if you'd left the heat on.

Grain & Bean Cooking Chart—Approximate Times

	Pressure Cooking (Unsoaked)	Stove-top Simmering (Soaked)
Grains		
Brown rice, short grain	15 to 17 minutes	35 minutes
Millet	Don't pressure cook	20 minutes
Wheat berries	35 minutes	1 hour
Rye berries	40 minutes	1 1/4 hours
Pearled barley	10 minutes	25 minutes
Beans		
Lentils	Don't pressure cook	20 minutes
Soybeans	30 minutes	2 1/2 to 3 hours
Kidney beans	22 to 25 minutes	1 1/2 to 2 hours
Pinto beans	22 to 25 minutes	1 1/2 to 2 hours
Chick peas	40 minutes	3 hours
Black beans	22 to 25 minutes	1 1/2 to 2 hours
Peanuts	40 minutes	3 hours

Granola

Granola is the name for any cereal made from roasted whole grains. I use all sorts of flakes, seeds, and nuts in my granola, then bake it with a very light honey and oil dressing.

Basic:
   4 cups oat flakes (rolled oats)
   2 cups rye flakes
   2 cups wheat flakes
   1 cup soy flakes
The more the better:
   1 cup sesame seeds, popped
   1 cup pumpkin seeds, popped
   1 cup sunflower seeds
   2 to 3 cups nuts, coarsely chopped (walnuts, almonds, cashews, peanuts)
   1 fresh coconut, smashed and grated, or 2 cups dried unsweetened coconut
   1 cup dried milk powder
Dressing:
   3/4 cup honey or maple syrup
   1/2 cup sesame or peanut oil
   1/2 cup water
   1 teaspoon pure vanilla extract
   1/2 to 1 pound dried fruits (raisins, currants, chopped dates)

1. Mix together all the dry ingredients in the biggest bowl you have. (Your bread bowl is perfect.) If 2 of you are making granola, one can do the popping while the other assembles everything else. I pop sesame and pumpkin seeds to give them a toastier flavor. Heat them slowly in an ungreased skillet, and they'll puff up and jump like popcorn. Stir frequently so the seeds don't burn, and keep a cover for the skillet handy so the seeds don't fly all over the kitchen when they start to pop. A fresh coconut is fun. Get a hammer and whack it to crack the husk. Drain out the coconut milk and drink it or save it for curry liquid. Peel off the husk. Then grate the pieces of white meat on the inside. The thin brown skin adhering to the meat is fine to grate up and eat too.

2. Warm the ingredients of the dressing together in a pot to blend them.

3. Pour the dressing over the grain and seed mixture, and stir it in with a big wooden spoon.

4. Oil shallow baking pans lightly. Scoop granola into them, and smooth the top so nothing will stick up and burn.

5. Bake for about 1 hour and 15 minutes in a 300 degrees F oven, stirring every 15 minutes so the granola doesn't burn on the bottom. You can bake it a longer or a shorter time to vary the crunch.

6. The minute granola comes out of the oven, mix in dried fruits. Never bake them in the oven with the flake-seed mixture or they will burn.

7. When it's cooked, store granola in a tightly closed glass jar, with a vanilla bean if you have one.

Variations:

—After you've made granola once, don't follow this recipe. Mix together any flakes, seeds, and nuts you like.

—Try adding a pinch of cinnamon and a pinch of nutmeg to the dressing.

Yield: Lots (about 1 gallon)

Whole Wheat Egg Pasta

Homemade whole wheat noodles will always be thicker than pasta you can buy, but you can't beat their fresh taste. Pasta-making is also the perfect therapy when you're mad. You start off growling at the world, but by the time your pasta is rolled out, you love everyone. All aggressions have been channeled into thin noodles.

If you grind your own flour, try to get durum wheat berries for pasta. Durum wheat is commonly called 'macaroni wheat.' It's used for pasta because it's hard and holds up well under boiling. You'll notice when you grind it that it shatters into tiny pieces, rather than grinding to powder as does hard red bread wheat. Grind durum wheat very fine, and pasta dough will be much easier to roll out. Forge ahead even if you can't get durum wheat: bread wheat makes good pasta dough too.

    2 cups whole wheat flour
    1/2 teaspoon sea salt
    2 eggs
    1/2 cup water (more or less)

1. Mix the flour together with the salt in a mound in the middle of a bread board or counter. Push aside a little of the mixture for kneading.
2. Make a well in the center of the flour, crack the eggs into it, and add a little water. Mix the eggs and the water with your fingertips, then mix together all the ingredients.
3. Now the work begins. Start kneading, and knead 15 minutes or until the dough is well-mixed and smooth. This will not be like kneading bread. Pasta dough is hard. If the dough is too dry and flaky, add more water: if it's too wet, add more flour.
4. Divide the dough into 2 sections. Flour your counter. Then using a sturdy rolling pin, preferably a solid one so you can really bash it around, flatten each piece of dough until it's as close to paper-thin as you can get it. Anything is permitted: you can smack the dough, shove it; eventually you'll roll it. I like to think of little Italian ladies doing this—how strong they must be. (This rolling can also be done very easily with a small hand-operated pasta-making machine.)

5. Cut each sheet of rolled dough into the shapes you choose. Lasagne noodles should be 1 1/2 to 2 inches wide. Big squares of pasta can be stuffed to make ravioli. Little squares are perfect for arranged pasta dishes. And pasta cut into strips about 1/4 inch wide is called fettuccine (little ribbons). Fettuccine is the most common form for pasta. It's good for tossed pasta dishes, like sinfully rich fettuccine.

6. Drape the noodles on a clean towel over the back of a chair to dry a little. I've heard it's traditional to string the noodles over a broom handle resting between 2 chairs.

7. You can cook the pasta while it's still fresh, before it's dried completely. Or leave the noodles you don't plan on using immediately to dry out thoroughly.

Variation:

—Green egg pasta—Instead of using water in the pasta dough, mix puréed or finely chopped greens in with the eggs. I like starting with about 1/2 pound of fresh greens—spinach, Swiss chard, basil leaves, or parsley. Or I start with 1 pint of frozen greens. Cook the greens until they're tender, then drain off the cooking water. (Save it in case you need more water while making pasta.) Mash the greens through a coarse sieve or a Foley food mill, or chop them up fine. Then add them as your pasta liquid. The pasta you get will not only be an organic-looking green color, but it will taste of the green it is made from.

Yield: Noodles for 4 to 6 people

How To Cook Pasta

1. Fill your largest pot about 2/3 full of water. Salt the water lightly, then bring it to a boil.

2. Add the pasta you want to cook along with a little oil to keep the noodles from sticking to each other. Let the water come to a boil again; stir the noodles with a metal or wooden fork to separate them; then cover the pot, turn off the heat, and leave the noodles cooking slowly.

3. Fresh, undried homemade noodles are cooked in about 7 minutes. Dried pasta cooks for a longer time, about 10 minutes. Pasta bought in a natural foods store is extra-dry, and needs about about 12 minutes to cook. Taste pasta along the way, however, to catch it at exactly the doneness you like. I prefer this method of cooking to rapid boiling because this way you have more control over how done the pasta gets.

4. Pour the cooked pasta into a collander to drain it. Save the pasta cooking water if you're going to make bread, because many of the water-soluble vitamins of the flour are in the cooking water.

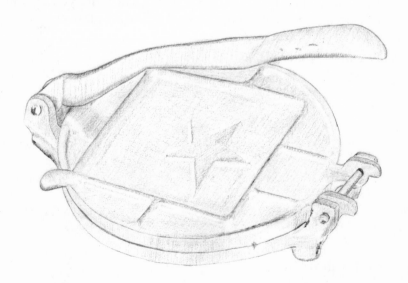

TORTILLA PRESS—I use my press to shape tortillas quickly.

Quick Fake Corn Tortillas

In Western United States good commercial tortillas are available everywhere, but on the East Coast they're almost impossible to find. Many cooks make authentic-tasting homemade tortillas from commercial masa harina (flour made from corn treated with limewater). I also like these 'fakes'. They're made from cornmeal and whole wheat flour, and have a deep grainy taste which complements robust Mexican fillings and sauces.

Serve tortillas while still warm, buttered or spread with guacamole. Pile them high with refried beans, cheese, olives, lettuce, and sour cream for tostadas. Or roll them around piquant fillings and cover them with red chile sauce for enchiladas.

    1 cup boiling water
    1 cup cornmeal, yellow, white, or blue
    1 teaspoon sea salt
    1 1/2 to 2 cups (more or less) whole wheat flour

1. Mix the cornmeal and salt in a bowl. Pour the boiling water over them, and let the mixture sit for about 10 minutes while the cornmeal soaks up the water.
2. Mix in whole wheat flour, a little at a time, until you have a good stiff dough. Make sure it's still moist, however. I sometimes add too much whole wheat flour, and have problems with the tortillas falling apart when I try to roll them out later.
3. Knead the dough a few minutes until it holds together.
4. Divide it into 12 balls, and roll the balls in your hands so they're smooth.
5. On a counter sprinkled with cornmeal, roll out each ball until it's about 6 inches in diameter and quite thin. Or press the balls in a tortilla press. (The dough will stick to the metal of the press, so I always lay the dough in the press between 2 sheets of waxed paper or between 2 halves torn from a sturdy plastic bag.)
6. Cook the tortillas on a lightly oiled skillet, flipping them once so they're lightly toasted on both sides. Don't cook them too long, or they'll be rock-hard and impossible to roll or fold.

Yield: 12 6-inch tortillas

Cornbread

A cake-like cornbread—moist and sweet with molasses. Delicious hot and buttered, served with soups.

    2 cups yellow cornmeal
    1 1/4 cups whole wheat pastry flour
    1/4 cup dry milk powder
    2 teaspoons baking soda
    2 teaspoons salt
    3 eggs
    1/2 cup molasses
    1/4 cup honey
    2 cups buttermilk or sour milk

1. Mix the dry ingredients in a bowl. Make a well in the center and crack in the eggs. Beat them with a fork, then beat in the molasses, honey, and buttermilk. (You need buttermilk or sour milk because the acid in them reacts with the baking soda to create carbon dioxide gas, which raises the bread. To make sour milk, add 2 tablespoons of lemon juice or vinegar to 2 cups of regular sweet milk.)
2. Slowly stir the liquids into the dry ingredients. Do not beat or overmix, since too much mixing will cause you to lose all the carbon dioxide gas.
3. Pour the mixture into a well-buttered, medium (about 9 to 10 inches) steep-sided cast iron skillet or a well-buttered 10 inch cake pan.
4. Bake in a 350 degree F oven for about 45 minutes, or until the cornbread is lightly browned on top and firm in the center.

Yield: 9 or 10 inch round cornbread

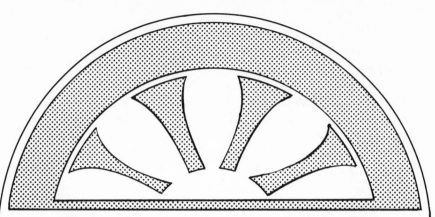

Raw Vegetables - Salads

Salads are the core of the vegetarian diet. You should use vegetables at their peak—fresh, ripe, and full-flavored. Salads will make you want to grow a garden. You'll need a big bowl. It must be very big so you can toss your salad vigorously without dribbling it on the floor. A sharp French chef's knife or a Japanese cleaver helps to cut vegetables cleanly. A good olive oil and a good red wine vinegar make a tasty dressing. And without at least one clove of garlic, you might as well forget about salads. The deep garlic taste turns a random assortment of vegetables into a sensuous, rich-flavored dish.

SALAD DRESSINGS

Vinaigrette Dressing

The lightest, freshest salad dressing.

  Olive oil
  Red wine vinegar
  Sea salt
  Freshly ground black pepper
  1 or 2 cloves garlic, mashed

1. Toss your whole salad with just enough olive oil to coat every piece. This coating keeps the greens from wilting, and protects the vitamins in the vegetables. All the nutrients of fresh vegetables remain in salads.
2. Make up the vinegar mixture—vinegar, salt, pepper, and mashed garlic. I like to put all the ingredients in a glass bottle with a tight cork or a tight-fitting lid, and shake them up. You can also mix the ingredients in a small bowl. I like using more vinegar than oil in my salads, but each person has a very different idea of what tastes best. Find out what suits you.
3. At the moment you're ready to eat the salad, shake or stir up the vinegar mixture again. Pour the dressing over the oil-coated salad, and toss it. Taste the salad for salt, and add a little more if it needs it.

An alternative method for using vinaigrette dressing:
1. Mix up the oil, vinegar, and seasonings in the bottom of your salad bowl. Marinate in the dressing all the fresh herbs you're using in the salad. (Lots of fresh herbs are delicious—minced parsley, chives, scallions, dill, basil, mint, marjoram....) Also marinate onions.
2. Break your greens and your other salad ingredients in on top of the dressing.
3. Right before you want to eat, toss the dressing up from the bottom of the bowl.

Variations:
—You can add other good tastes to the vinegar mixture—fresh lemon juice, red wine, dried herbs, homemade mayonnaise or ricotta cheese, and dried mustard.

Homemade Mayonnaise

I use homemade mayonnaise on open face sandwiches, in salads, and as a dip for steamed artichoke leaves. I also mix it with vinegar to make what I call 'rugged dressing.' Homemade mayonnaise is thick, creamy, and lemon-yellow colored, with the rich taste mayonnaise should have.

Mayonnaise is a fascinating food. Normally oil and vinegar won't stay mixed. But in mayonnaise the egg yolk mixes with the vinegar, and spreads out to coat tiny droplets of oil and keep them separated. (You break the oil into droplets by beating it rapidly.) Since the oil droplets cannot join together to form larger droplets which would settle out, the oil is thus suspended in the egg-vinegar liquid.

You can use whole eggs to make mayonnaise. But egg whites just dilute the coating ability of the yolks, so whole eggs are not as good at forming films with vinegar as egg yolks alone.

I like using sesame or olive oils best for mayonnaise, but any unrefined oil will do. Right after you make it, homemade mayonnaise will taste strongly of the oil from which it's made; the taste will get milder with aging.

It's important to have all the ingredients at room temperature when you start making mayonnaise. Warm oil is much easier to break into droplets, and warm egg yolks form the fastest films. Choose a large mixing bowl so oil won't spatter all over, and use a wire whisk for beating. Mayonnaise is perfect for two people to make. One adds the oil, and the other beats.

> 2 egg yolks
> 1/2 teaspoon sea salt
> 1/2 teaspoon red wine vinegar
> Pinch dry mustard
> 1 cup unrefined oil
> 1 1/2 tablespoons vinegar or juice of 1/2 lemon

1. Whisk the egg yolks in a bowl until they're creamy lemon colored.
2. Beat the salt, 1/2 teaspoon red wine vinegar, and the mustard into the yolks.

3. Whisk in vigorously about 1/2 cup of oil, *adding it very slowly*—
drop by drop at first, then in a slow trickle. If 2 people are making
mayonnaise, one person can add the oil and one beat; then switch.
Pausing is actually beneficial. When you're not beating, the egg-
vinegar solution which isn't already coating oil droplets will
coalesce into a layer. This layer films new droplets of oil more
easily than if you hadn't allowed the layer to form.
4. Nothing will seem to happen for quite awhile. Then gradually
you'll notice that the mixture is thickening up. The emulsion has
'taken'; you can relax.
5. Now add the remaining oil in a more steady stream, alternating
with the 1 1/2 tablespoons vinegar or lemon juice.
6. Taste and reseason. Put your finished mayonnaise in a glass jar
and keep it in the refrigerator.

What to do with mayonnaise that breaks (doesn't take):
Don't despair. If your mayonnaise didn't thicken up, start over. Get
a new egg yolk. Warm it to room temperature. Whisk it until it's
creamy lemon colored. Now add the oil-egg mixture from your
unsuccessful try, drop by drop, whisking heartily. Keep going.

If that doesn't work, use the oil-egg-vinegar mixture for salad
dressing, just as it is, or with a little more vinegar added.

Variations:
—Sesame mayonnaise—If you're using sesame oil, add 1 tablespoon
sesame butter or 2 generous tablespoons sesame meal (sesame seeds
ground up in a grain mill) for a real sesame taste.
—Green mayonnaise—Whisk about 1/2 cup of finely minced fresh
parsley or watercress or any mixture of fresh green herbs into
your finished mayonnaise.

Yield: 1 1/4 cups

Garlic Mayonnaise (Aioli)

Classically in France, aioli is served as a dip for raw and lightly steamed vegetables. I also use it as a base for open face sandwiches and as a salad dressing, especially for salads with lots of tomatoes in them. You might add even more garlic than is called for in this recipe.

    6 to 8 cloves garlic, mashed
    1/2 teaspoon sea salt
    2 egg yolks
    1/2 teaspoon red wine vinegar
    1 cup unrefined oil
    Juice 1 lemon

Follow directions in the homemade mayonnaise recipe. Add the garlic with the salt.

Variation:
—Green garlic mayonnaise—Whisk about 1/2 cup of finely minced fresh green herbs into your finished mayonnaise.

Yield: 1 1/4 cups

Rugged Dressing

This creamy dressing can be made very quickly if you've made mayonnaise first. I call it 'rugged dressing' because you can make it as sharp as you like with vinegar and black pepper. A friend tasted my dressing, breathed hard, and said, 'Yow, is that rugged! But I like it.' You can also make it very mild and smooth by whisking in cream. I like serving this dressing in a pitcher so each person can pour it.

  2 parts plain or garlic mayonnaise, green or yellow
  1 part red wine vinegar
  Freshly ground black pepper
  Thick cream

1. Whisk the mayonnaise with the vinegar until no lumps are left. Whisk in black pepper.
2. Taste.
3. If it knocks you over, whisk in some cream, and taste again.

Yoghurt Tahini Dressing

Simple and creamily delicious—tasting of garlic, the zings of yoghurt and lemon juice, and the rich sweetness of sesame. Yoghurt tahini dressing tastes good on all salads, and especially on salads with raisins.

  2 parts yoghurt
  1 part tahini
  fresh lemon juice
  garlic, mashed
  sea salt
  finely chopped fresh parsley

Mix the yoghurt and tahini. Add all the other ingredients to taste.

WHAT GOES IN SALADS

Greens

Swiss chard
My favorite summer salad green. It's flavorful and sturdy, a good
carrier for all the fresh herbs I like. Swiss chard's dark green color
shows it's high in Vitamin A, and thus is better for you than
lettuce. One planting of Swiss chard will provide you with salads all
spring, all summer, and well into the fall: as long as you keep
picking the leaves, they'll keep growing back. Pick the leaves when
they're small, about two to four inches tall.

Spinach
Always a delicious salad green, and high in Vitamin A. I buy
spinach for salads in the winter.

Fresh herbs
All fresh green herbs are tasty in salads. I use lots of parsley, chives,
fresh basil leaves, fresh mint, summer savory, marjoram, watercress,
and dill. Chop up whole scallions, the greens as well as the bottoms.

Lettuces
I like the tender round leaves of Boston lettuce. Romaine lettuce
(also called Cos) is a good crunch. If I have old faithful iceberg
lettuce, I like to mix it half and half with spinach. Alone, iceberg
seems too pale, but a dark and light mixture catches my eye. Try
red lettuce sometime for a really colorful salad.

Cabbage
Chinese cabbage is succulent, with a slightly sweet tangy flavor.
Green cabbage is a traditional crisp addition to salads. Coarsely
shredded red cabbage is beautiful in dark green salads.

Dandelion leaves
In the early spring young leaves make an excellent green, especially
if you toss one or two chopped hard-cooked eggs and some
crumbled bleu cheese into your salad.

Other Raw Vegetables

Traditionals
Red and white radishes, cucumbers, green peppers, sweet red peppers, carrots, and celery.

Asparagus
Comes out early in the season, and is tender and sweet eaten raw.

Fresh mushrooms
If you haven't tried them, it may seem unusual to eat raw mushrooms. Once you've tasted them, however, you'll probably never again have mushrooms left for cooking. Slice mushrooms thick so you can appreciate their succulent texture.

Peas
Fresh-shelled green peas are very sweet and bright green. Snow peas (edible pod peas) are good raw in salads if you pick them young.

Beets
Cut them in little cubes or in 'shoe strings'. I also like beets steamed until they're just tender, then cut.

Snap beans
I steam green and yellow snap beans before using them in salads. Raw they're not as tasty.

Broccoli
Pleasantly nutty raw. It's also good lightly steamed, especially in salads with cheese and cooked grains.

Cauliflower
Delicious raw in salads with yoghurt tahini dressing or in salads with toasted sesame seeds.

Summer squash
Both zucchini and yellow summer squash are much like cucumber raw, but more flavorful.

Jerusalem artichoke
Dice these tubers for a nutty crunch.

Onions
Sweet red and white onions are a snappy flavor.

Sprouts
Use all kinds of sprouts to make winter salads.

Fruits

Tomatoes
Tomatoes are bright red and juicy in salads. So are cherry
tomatoes.

Avocados
Sliced avocado transforms any salad into smooth tropical luxury.
Be sure the slices are big, so you know the avocados are there. See
the Index for buying and ripening avocados.

Orange and grapefruit sections
Citrus fruits have a sweet juiciness which goes surprisingly well in
salads. I use orange sections during the winter when tomatoes
are out of season. Don't mix tomatoes and citrus fruits together in
one salad, as their flavors clash.

Apples
Good in the fall. Cubes of apple and cubes of Cheddar cheese the
same size are a treat in salads. Use some homemade mayonnaise in
the dressing for apple salads.

And There's Still More

These ingredients sink to the bottom of your salad bowl, no matter how much you toss. With sunflower seeds, brown rice, cheese... added, a salad becomes a whole meal.

Nuts
Nuts are rich in salads. Try pine nuts, almonds, walnuts, and cashews. Leave them in big pieces.

Dried fruits
Raisins and dried currants are sweet surprises.

Seeds
All toasted seeds—sesame, sunflower, pumpkin—are delicious in salads, especially in salads with raisins.

Grains and beans
Toasted wheat germ is sweet and nutty. Cooked brown rice and wheat berries are a good chew. Cook up wheat or rye flakes for instant salad grains. Cooked lentils, chick peas, kidney beans, or any other beans give salads body. Beans are especially good in salads with lots of fresh dill. Cooked potatoes, diced with their skins on, have the same filling quality as grains and beans.

Cheese
I use cottage cheese to make dense salads. Ricotta cheese smooths out sharp tastes. Cubes of feta cheese are wonderfully salty and chewable. Use feta in salads with black olives and lemon juice dressing. Crumbled bleu cheese is almost a must in salads with raw mushrooms, and a taste which I enjoy in all salads. I like lots of hard cheese, especially Cheddar or Swiss, grated or diced. Aged Parmesan or Romano is good freshly grated on the coarse side of your grater, so you can taste the strong-flavored pieces.

Hard-cooked eggs
Cut eggs in quarters. Slices fall apart completely. In salads with lots of fresh herbs or greens which might be bitter, I've found that one hard-cooked egg chopped in works miracles. The egg mellows the herbs or greens so you can enjoy their flavors without even a hint of the bitterness you might taste otherwise.

Croutons

Toss these in at the last minute so they stay crisp. See the Index for a recipe.

Special items

Capers are salty with an exotic flowery taste. Try pickling nasturtium buds for a homemade alternative. Pimentos are bright red, and their taste complements that of capers. I like ripened black olives. Unripened green ones aren't as flavorful. Marinated mushrooms are surprisingly easy to make. Marinated artichoke hearts are luscious.

PREPARING VEGETABLES

Wash all the dirty greens and vegetables quickly with cold water. Then shake them in a colander and pat them with a clean towel to dry them thoroughly. If there's anything that can ruin a good salad, it's water coating everything and forming a little puddle at the bottom of your salad bowl or salad plates. To dry greens I particularly recommend a lettuce swinger. They're wire mesh baskets you fill with greens, then swing around to spin off all the water. If you wash greens immediately after you pick them and aren't going to use them right away, spin or shake them just a little, so they're still moist. Then lay them flat on top of each other and wrap them gently in a clean towel. Keep them in the refrigerator, and they will be crisp and ready-to-use when you open the towel.

Cutting vegetables is really an art. Each vegetable has spent its lifetime becoming the shape and color it is; and if you look at it carefully, you can see the way it would look best divided up. Respect it; don't massacre it. And cut each piece of a vegetable large enough that you can still tell what it is. I like using a sharp French chef's knife or a sharp Japanese cleaver.

Tear greens into mouthsize pieces.

Watercress and parsley and most fresh herbs can be snipped up with kitchen scissors. They should be in small pieces, or they will be stringy and choke you. Fresh basil leaves can be left whole.

Cabbage in mixed salads should be chopped in fairly large pieces or coarsely shredded. You lose its texture if you shred it fine as for cole slaw.

Carrots are definitely better sliced than grated: make them either rounds or slice them diagonally so you have ovals.

The stems of broccoli are sweet right down to where they become woody. Slice stems as well as flowerettes. That goes for cauliflower too. It pains me to see people throw away the best part of a vegetable.

Zucchini and yellow summer squash should be cut in thin slices.

Sweet onions should be thinly sliced.

Use tomato wedges rather than slices: slices fall apart.

SERVING SALADS

Salad Bar

Put your mixed salad greens in a big bowl, then arrange separate bowls of other chopped vegetables around the greens. Also fill bowls with chopped hard-cooked eggs, homemade croutons, crumbled bleu cheese, grated Parmesan cheese, toasted sunflower seeds, and marinated chick peas or any marinated vegetable. These are satisfying sprinklings guests can add to salads. For a selection of dressings, I'd recommend a cruet of olive oil and a cruet of the vinaigrette vinegar mixture, and a bowl of a creamy dressing such as yoghurt tahini dressing, which will stay on top of a salad rather than swimming around each person's plate or bowl. People using salad bars often prefer creamy dressings.

Give everyone a big soup bowl, a big wooden bowl, or a big plate to make an individual salad exactly as he or she wants. Big plates are essential: no one can make a decent salad in a tiny space.

Tossed Wooden Bowl Salads

Wooden bowl salads are a million to one my favorite. Nothing else approaches the taste of fresh vegetables and sprinklings tossed together with dressing evenly coating it all.

I treat my salad bowl with great respect, and I think the bowl makes better salads for it. I always start making a wooden bowl salad by peeling a clove of garlic and slicing it in half. Then I pour a little olive oil into the bottom of my salad bowl, and rub it all around the inside with the cut sides of the garlic. This seasons the bowl and keeps any liquids from soaking into the grain of the wood and ruining it. When we've finished eating, I wash the salad bowl quickly. I never soak it in water: that would be a fast way to destroy it.

You can really put anything you want into a tossed salad. Here are some suggestions to give you an idea of just how versatile salads can be, and to inspire you to toss up spontaneous combinations.

Classic Spinach Salad

An enticing blend of vegetables and cheese. This salad goes well with white wine.

Fresh spinach leaves
Sliced raw mushrooms
Tiny crisp homemade croutons
Cubes of Swiss cheese
Garlic rugged dressing

German Cucumber Salad

The trick to making German salad is to slice cucumbers and tomatoes so thin your grandmother would be proud of you. The German Grandmother who taught me to make it was a tyrant. 'It is impossible for Americans to make German salad,' she told me when I tried.

Eat mit dense pumpernickel, which can be dunked in the salad juice, and with big slices of holy Swiss cheese.

Cucumbers, sliced
Firm ripe tomatoes, sliced
Homemade mayonnaise
Lemon juice
Lots of freshly ground black pepper

Sprinkle this salad with chopped scallions, and chill it. The salad gets better with sitting, so make it as early as you want.

Early Summer Salad

Green peas are sweet little morsels in salad.

    Freshly shelled green peas
    Leaf lettuce
    Sliced radishes
    Scallions
    Grated Cheddar cheese
    Wheat germ
    Vinaigrette dressing

Lunch Salad

Dense and nourishing, this salad is a whole meal.

    Swiss chard
    Scallions and lots of other fresh green herbs
    Cottage cheese
    Cooked brown rice
    Yoghurt tahini dressing
    (Walnuts optional)

Linda Fisher Salad

Garlicky and full of other exciting strong tastes. This salad is
dedicated to Linda Fisher, the only person I know to have ever
burned hard-cooked eggs.

    Hard-cooked eggs
    Lettuces of all sorts
    Watercress
    Fresh parsley
    Tomatoes
    Carrots
    Scallions
    Capers and pimentos
    Garlicky, garlicky dressing
    Very old, very ripe Parmesan cheese grated on top

Hammondsport Salad

Wildly extravagant and festive, this salad has almost all my favorite foods in it, including bleu cheese. Good with straightforward foods, like millet soufflé, cheese quiche, or a slice of homemade bread.

  Fresh spinach leaves
  Raw cauliflowerettes
  1 or 2 carrots, sliced
  Oranges, sectioned with sections cut in half
  Handful sunflower seeds, toasted in a pan
  Raisins
  A good crumbling of bleu cheese
  Vinaigrette dressing
  (Sliced mushrooms optional)

Orange & Onion Salad

Unusual, with a taste of tarragon.

  1 small onion, diced
  1 orange, sectioned with sections cut in half
  Olive oil
  Red wine vinegar
  Tarragon
  Sea salt
  Freshly ground black pepper
  Salad greens
  Cucumber, sliced
  Scallions
  (Sliced avocado optional)

1. Marinate the onion, orange, and salad dressing ingredients in the bottom of your salad bowl for about 1 hour.
2. Break the salad greens, sliced cucumber, scallions and avocado in on top of the dressing.
3. Right before you want to eat, toss the dressing up from the bottom.

Evolution Salad

A delicious salad with fruits, avocado, and sour cream. Good with millet soufflé, cheese fondue, or Mim's Turkish eggplant.

Sturdy lettuce, like Romaine
Grapefruit sections
Bananas, sliced
Avocado, sliced
Dressing:
    1/2 cup sour cream
    2 teaspoons honey
    Juice 1/2 lime
    1/2 teaspoon curry powder

1. Peel and section the grapefruit and remove membranes from sections. Efficient way—Slice off the top rind so you can see the grapefruit; with a knife, saw off the rind and white in a spiral; cut off the bottom rind; and cut out segments between membranes. Inefficient but tasty way—Peel the grapefruit like an orange; somehow by artful pulling of membranes and prying of pulp extricate sections, nibbling all the while.
2. Mix together the ingredients of the dressing, and adjust everything to taste.
3. Right before you eat, toss the salad and the dressing.

Panchito's Salad

In the oven heat refried beans covered with Monterey Jack or Cheddar cheese. Prepare a salad of your favorite greens and top it with a generous mound of guacamole. Spoon the hot beans gently over the guacamole so the cheese is still on top. Sprinkle with alfalfa sprouts. Serve immediately.

SPECIAL SALADS

Marinade

A juicy marinade for vegetables and beans. Red wine vinegar and cider vinegar are both good. Olive, sesame, and peanut oils have the heartiest flavors and are tastiest for this kind of salad. Vary the sharpness of the marinade by changing the proportion of vinegar to oil.

3/4 to 1 cup vinegar
1/3 to 1/2 cup unrefined oil
2 or more cloves garlic, mashed
1 parsley root, chopped, or 3 or 4 sprigs fresh parsley, minced
Half a bay leaf
4 or 5 whole peppercorns
1/2 teaspoon sea salt

Mix together the ingredients in a saucepan, then boil them for 5 minutes.

Variations:
—Stir-fry 2 or 3 diced onions in butter in the saucepan before you add the other ingredients. Then mix in the rest of the marinade and boil it.
—Add herbs and spices to fit the vegetables you've chosen. A little oregano or thyme added to the boiling marinade is good with everything. A nice pour of sherry goes with everything too. Lots of fresh dill goes with marinated beans or beets. In general be daring seasoning the marinade.

Yield: 1 1/2 cups marinade. Enough for 1 pound vegetables

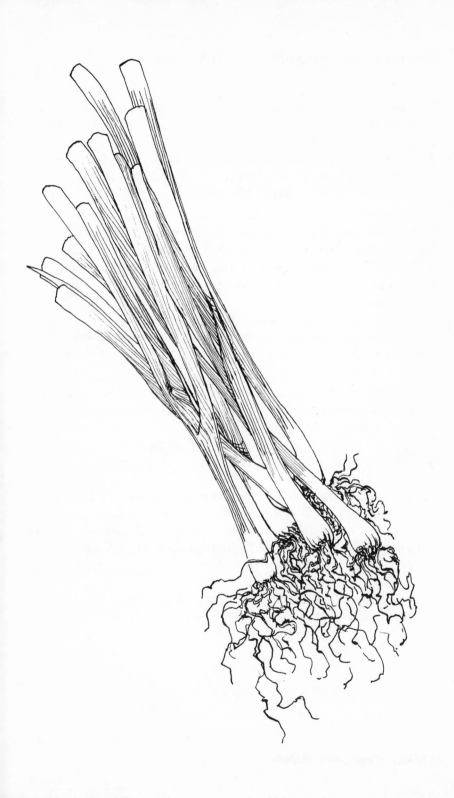

Marinated Vegetable & Bean Salads

Marinated salads are chunkier and heartier than tossed salads. You start out with whatever vegetables are in season—any one vegetable or several together. You mix in any beans you have cooked up. Then you pour a herby marinade over the salad, and let it steep. I like serving marinated salads on the side of open face sandwich plates and taking them on picnics.

1. Clean the vegetables and cut them into uniform big pieces.
2. Steam each of the following vegetables you're using until just tender: cauliflowerettes, carrot ovals, broccoli flowerettes and ovals, zucchini spears, eggplant cubes, beet cubes or shoe strings, snapped green or wax beans, asparagus spears, leek slices, whole mushrooms, artichokes.
These vegetables can be marinated raw: green and red bell pepper rings, sweet red and white onion rings, sliced radishes, chunks of red cabbage, big thick tomato slices (best if marinated with lots of onion rings).

3. Put the vegetables, steamed or raw, in a non-metal bowl. Stir in any cooked beans you wish to marinate. Chick peas, kidney beans, and soybeans are especially good.
4. Make the marinade. (See recipe on preceding page)
5. While the marinade is still hot, pour it over the vegetables and beans in the bowl.
6. Melt just a tad of butter over everything and stir it in. (You won't believe what a difference just a little butter makes.)
7. Leave the mixture covered in the refrigerator to marinate. Leave it anywhere from overnight to 24 hours, turning it with a big spoon every now and then so all the vegetables get a chance to soak in the marinade.
8. Before serving the salad, toss in lots of snipped fresh parsley, chives, or scallions, and sprinkle more on top for color.

Marinated Mushrooms

My favorite marinated salad. If you can restrain yourself, leave the mushrooms marinating at room temperature for four to five days. They steep in an essence of fennel and coriander.

   1 pound whole mushrooms
   Marinade (See recipe on preceding page)
   Additions to marinade:
      1/2 teaspoon dried thyme
      10 fennel seeds
      10 coriander seeds or 1/2 teaspoon ground coriander

1. Wash the mushrooms, and boil them for about 4 minutes in salted water. Pour off the water and toss the mushrooms dry in the hot pan. Put them in a non-metal bowl.
2. Make the marinade, adding the herbs and spices listed above.
3. While it's still hot, pour the marinade over the mushrooms.
4. Leave them at room temperature for 4 to 5 days, turning them occasionally with a big spoon.
5. When they're ready, either use the mushrooms right away or keep them in a jar in the refrigerator.

Yield: 1 quart

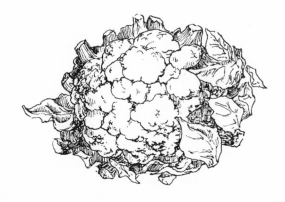

Potato Salad

My mother taught me the trick for making a really tasty potato
salad. You dice the potatoes right after they're cooked and while
they're still hot, then marinate them overnight in oil, vinegar, and
herbs. The next day you add the rest of the ingredients. Mom has
also found that the best potatoes to cook for a good-textured
potato salad are small to medium-size older potatoes (not new
potatoes). I leave potato skins on—for their color, for their vitamins
and minerals, and for sheer orneriness: I will never peel a potato. (I
do scrub the potatoes with a stiff-bristled brush before cooking
them.)

    6 medium potatoes
    Marinade:
        2 tablespoons unrefined oil
        6 tablespoons red wine vinegar
        Finely minced fresh herbs or a mixture of fresh and dried
            herbs (parsley, chives, dill, scallions, basil, thyme, or
            tarragon)
    Add the second day:
        2 medium onions, diced
        2 or 3 stalks celery, diced
        2 hard-cooked eggs, diced
        Homemade mayonnaise
        Salt and pepper

1. Put the unpeeled scrubbed potatoes in a pot and cover them
with salted water. Bring the water to a boil, cover the pot, and
simmer until the potatoes are just tender, about 20 to 25 minutes
depending on their size. Don't overcook them.
2. Pour off the potato water, and save it for bread.
3. As soon as the potatoes are cool enough to handle, dice them
into bite-sized cubes.
4. In a bowl toss the potato cubes lightly with just enough
marinade to coat the cubes. Be very gentle so you don't break up
the potatoes. You're aiming for a salad of good, firm cubes, not
mashed potatoes. Cover the salad bowl with a plate and leave the
salad overnight in the refrigerator to marinate.

5. The next day mix in the onions, celery, and hard-cooked eggs. Toss in homemade mayonnaise until the salad is moist, then add salt and pepper to taste.

6. Garnish the salad with red onion rings or sliced radishes, then sprinkle it with paprika and finely minced fresh parsley.

Variations:
—Add diced sweet green or red peppers on the second day.
—Dilly bean and potato salad—Mix in lots of snapped green or wax beans, steamed until just tender, along with the celery. Add lots of fresh dill.
—Scandinavian-style beet and potato salad—On the first day mix in cubes of cooked beet and lots of fresh dill and chives to marinate with the potatoes. Serve the salad with slices of hard-cooked egg on top.

Yield: Serves 4 to 6

Cole Slaw

Cole slaw is the perfect winter salad, especially if you're trying to grow most of your own vegetables. Cabbage will keep all winter stored in your basement, and is a good winter source of Vitamin C. Cabbage also has that succulent crunch which you crave when there aren't many fresh vegetables around. You can make simple cole slaw, or if you enjoy creating, cole slaw can be almost as free-style as tossed wooden bowl salads. I prefer cider vinegar on cole slaw. It's full and fruity.

> Green cabbage, grated
> Onion, grated or finely chopped
> Unrefined oil (Olive is best.)
> Sea salt
> Black pepper
> Cider vinegar

1. Shred the cabbage with a carrot peeler, grate it on a grater, or chop it up fine with a knife. Grate or chop the onion.
2. Using 2 forks, toss the cabbage and onions with just enough oil to coat them. Sprinkle with salt and pepper, and toss again.
3. Toss in vinegar, then taste and reseason.

Variations:
—If the salad is a bit tart, add some raisins or dried currants. Or start some raisins soaking in the vinegar before you make the salad, so the vinegar you use will be slightly sweet.
—Cole slaw just means cabbage salad, so as long as you put some cabbage in it, there's no limit as to what else you can shred up and add. In one salad shred everything about the same size, but experiment with different coarsenesses of shredding in different salads. Try adding red cabbage, green peppers, carrots, radishes, beets, and fresh horseradish. For different flavors, snip in parsley, scallions, chives, fresh mint, or fresh dill. Add mashed garlic for a deeper taste. A little celery seed, caraway seed, or finely minced capers perks up simple cole slaw.
—Chunks of fresh pineapple, orange sections, grated fresh coconut, or chunks of apple can be added to make fruity slaws.
—Here are a few suggestions for alternate dressings. Homemade mayonnaise mixed with a little vinegar is smoother and richer than

an oil and vinegar dressing. Sour cream is the delicatessan cole slaw secret. Mix it with mayonnaise, then add lemon juice, salt, and pepper. A sour cream and maple syrup dressing will make a delicious sweet cole slaw. A nutty cole slaw dressing is made from peanut butter mixed with yoghurt, fresh lemon juice, a little honey, and sea salt. Use it on cole slaws with grated carrots, lots of chopped nuts, and raisins.

—Apple cole slaw is an infallible fall salad. Mix coarsely chopped cabbage with chopped celery, unpeeled red apples diced up, lots of raisins, and homemade mayonnaise.

Tabbouleh

Tabbouleh is a salad full of the wonderful chew of bulghur and the fresh tastes of lemon and tomatoes, fresh parsley, and fresh mint. Stuff pockets of Arabic bread with tabbouleh, or eat it with your fingers, using Arabic bread for pincers. I especially like serving tabbouleh on plates with Arabic bread, hummus, and baba ganoush.

    1 cup dry bulghur
    2 cups water
    2 medium onions, finely chopped
    1 cup finely chopped fresh mint leaves
    3 cups finely chopped fresh parsley
    1 or 2 large tomatoes, chopped
    1/4 cup olive oil
    Juice 2 lemons
    1 teaspoon sea salt
    Freshly ground black pepper

1. Soak the bulghur in water for about 2 hours or until all the water is absorbed.
2. Mix in the onions, crushing them into the wheat.
3. Toss in the mint, parsley, tomatoes, olive oil, and lemon juice. Stir in the salt and pepper, and taste.

Variations:
—You can vary the amounts of parsley and mint you add to suit your taste.

Yield: Serves 6 to 8

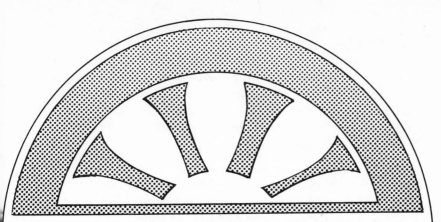

Cooked Vegetables

One of the reasons many people don't find vegetables exciting is the traditional American way of preparing them: vegetables are dumped in too much water and overcooked. They lose their taste, color, and much of their nutritive value. There are two cooking techniques which avoid these pitfalls, both commonly used in the Orient but as yet rarely used here. The one I prefer is stir-frying. The other is steaming.

A vegetable stir-fry is almost a hot salad: you clean and cut fresh vegetables as for salad, then fry them quickly in hot oil with a little water, tamari sauce, or sherry. Since the outside of each vegetable is seared in oil, the juices and vitamins are sealed inside and protected, and you preserve the distinct flavor, the bright color, and the nutritive value of the vegetable.

Steaming is a good method for cooking vegetables with complex or flowery shapes, since it surrounds the whole vegetable with steam. Especially good vegetables for steaming are broccoli, cauliflower, asparagus, corn-on-the-cob, and the noble artichoke.

STEAMING

1. Put vegetables in a small steaming basket made of bamboo or metal (available in Oriental stores or specialty cooking shops). For an improvised steaming basket, use a metal colander.
2. Place the basket over a small amount of water (about 1/2 inch deep) in a pot with a tight-fitting lid.
3. Cover the pot, and bring the water to a boil. The vegetables will cook in the steam from the boiling water.
4. Open the pot and test for tenderness by sticking a fork in the vegetables. Remove them from the steamer when they're bright-colored and tender.
5. Always save the water in the bottom of the pot for bread or soups.

Artichokes

The best method for cooking artichokes is to steam them in a pressure cooker. (I would never cook other vegetables in the pressure cooker, however, as it is much too easy to overcook them.) I serve hot steamed artichokes with a bowl of homemade mayonnaise, melted butter, or melted lemon butter for a dip. To melt butter, put it in a small dish on top of the pressure cooker as the artichokes cook. To make lemon butter, add a squirt of fresh lemon juice.

I think hot steamed artichokes are filling enough to be served as a main dish. I cook one big artichoke for each person, and serve it with salad and homemade bread.

1. Put about 1/4 to 1/2 inch of water in the cooker and salt it lightly. Put in the cooker rack.
2. Clean the artichokes, and place them on the rack.
3. Cover the cooker, and put on the 15 pound pressure gauge. Heat until the gauge starts to rock or jiggle, then adjust the heat so the gauge rocks gently or jiggles about once a minute.
4. Cook for 15 minutes.
5. Bring down the pressure, and remove the artichokes.

STIR-FRYING

1. Cutting is crucial for stir-fried vegetables. Cut your vegetables before you start cooking, since once you start stir-frying, it goes very fast. Keep all vegetable pieces about the same size and same general shape. This is essential for even cooking.

2. Heat your stir-frying pan over fairly high heat. There's only 1 inflexible requirement for a stir-frying pan: it must be big enough that you can stir your vegetables. Many people use woks, traditional Chinese stir-frying pans. Woks have sloping sides, and you can get specially shaped wok spatulas for stirring the vegetables. The best woks are the heavy ones made of tempered steel. I like stir-frying vegetables in a big, steep-sided, cast-iron skillet. I stir the vegetables with a wooden spoon or with chopsticks.

3. Pour in about 1 or 2 tablespoons of unrefined oil. You need only a little oil to keep your vegetables from sticking, but its taste is very important. I generally prefer the flavors of peanut or sesame oil in stir-fries. Olive oil is good, and a mixture of olive oil and butter is extraordinarily good.

4. Stir-fry onions, herbs, and seeds first to give the stir-fry a deep baseline flavor. As soon as the oil sizzles, add onions, mashed garlic, and minced fresh ginger, or as many of them as you're using. Stir-fry about 2 minutes. Then add dried herbs and seeds. A good herb mixture for stir-fries is rosemary, thyme, and basil. Sesame seeds are good in any stir-fry. Stir constantly for about 2 minutes more.

5. Now add your vegetables. Add vegetables with the hardest, densest textures first. Stir them rapidly around the pan, then put a cover on the pan to steam them for a few minutes. Next add the softer vegetables, and stir them in similarly. Turn down the heat under the pan as the cooking progresses. If the vegetables start to stick, pour in a little water or tamari sauce. A good dash of sherry never hurt a stir-fry. Continue adding softer vegetables, stirring rapidly and covering the pan for a few minutes, then stirring more until all your vegetables are in the pan. A vegetable cooking chart is at the end of the chapter.

6. Warning: do not overcook vegetables. Cook the stir-fry until each vegetable is just-done—crispy, bright-colored, and strong-

tasting. Never cook a vegetable until it's pale, soft, or mushy.

7. Wipe your pan out with a cloth or rinse it lightly. Your pan will stay seasoned if you don't scrub it. Everything you make in it will taste better, and you'll never have to use much oil.

8. Serve stir-fried vegetables as a side dish, or serve them over grains or pasta for a whole meal.

Some Nice Vegetable Combinations

Each vegetable tastes good stir-fried alone. The earth is also kind to us: vegetables in season at the same time always go exceptionally well together. Really, try any combination your taste dictates.

Asparagus spears, mushrooms cut in half, and spinach; fried in butter with lemon juice and salt

Cauliflower in flowerettes, carrot ovals, and snow peas; fried in sesame oil and butter, with bright green scallions cut in 1 inch tubes sprinkled over the top

Onions and green peppers, diced, potato slices, and eggplant cubes: fried in olive oil with ground coriander seeds or minced fresh coriander leaves

Lots of onion and green pepper rings, slices of zucchini and yellow summer squash; fried in peanut oil with rosemary and fresh marjoram; served with sesame onion sauce (See Index)

Green and red cabbage, very coarsely shredded; fried in butter with caraway seeds

Onions, diced, mushrooms in slices, and snap beans; fried with lots of garlic, fresh dill, and tamari sauce

Broccoli is one of the best stir-fried vegetables, by itself in peanut oil or butter, or with fresh ginger and tamari sauce.

ADDITIONS TO STIR-FRIED VEGETABLES

These additions radically change the taste and texture of the dish.

Tamari and soy sauce are both made from soybeans fermented with wheat and salt. The two sauces taste different because different bacteria do the fermenting. Most natural foods cooks recommend using tamari sauce because many of the soy sauces available today are fakes: the soybeans are not fermented at all, but are broken down rapidly by acids. As far as I know, all tamari sauces are the real thing. Tamari sauce is available in all natural foods stores, and has a rich winey taste you'll enjoy trying. If you buy soy sauce, try to get real Oriental brands.

You can find interesting fresh and dried vegetables and soybean products in Chinese markets. Soak dried ingredients in water or in Charlotte's master sauce (See page 216) before you add them to stir-fried vegetables. Dried black mushrooms, black fungus, day lily buds, and soybean skins are all unusual textures. Dried seaweeds give stir-fries a salty, close-to-the-ocean flavor.

Almonds and fresh pineapple cubes added to vegetables make a tasty stir-fry. Fresh water chestnuts, peeled and sliced, are sweet and crunchy. Chips of fresh coconut are another sweet taste. Bean threads, transparent slippery strands of mung bean starch, are strange but seductive. Soak them before you add them.

Tofu (soybean curd) is almost indispensable in stir-fries once you've tasted it. Cut tofu in 1/2-inch cubes, and add it along with extra tamari to keep it from sticking. (See Index)

A Japanese touch is to toss in a little rice wine vinegar right before the stir-fry is finished cooking. It accents all the vegetable flavors. Red wine vinegar does the same trick.

Nuts of all sorts—cashews, walnuts, hazlenuts—enrich stir-fries, as do nut and seed butters.

Crack one or two eggs into a bowl, beat them lightly, then pour them over the stir-fry as soon as the vegetables finish cooking. Stir the eggs in quickly.

Add cooked grains or pasta to the stir-fry. Along with them add extra liquids so the grains won't stick. Pasta stir-fried with butter and cabbage is especially good.

Sprinkle a few handfuls of grated cheese over the vegetables in the stir-fry pan, and pop the pan under the broiler. The cheese melts down through the stir-fry and some lingers tantalizingly on the surface.

Mix sour cream or yoghurt with grated mild cheese and with chopped chives or other minced fresh herbs. Smooth the sauce over the stir-fry and heat it in the oven.

For other sauces, see the Sauces chapter.

Julie's Favorite Stir-Fry

A little bit of everything, with lots of garlic, rosemary, and sesame seeds. Serve with brown rice, a good mound of cottage cheese, and tamari sauce. Or serve it with a big baked potato and sour cream.

1 to 2 teaspoons sesame or peanut oil
2 medium onions, sliced
3 or more cloves garlic, mashed
1/2 teaspoon dried rosemary, crushed
1 tablespoon sesame seeds
2 large carrots, sliced diagonally
2 stalks broccoli, slices and flowerettes
Cauliflowerettes
1 handful mushrooms, sliced in thick slices
1 handful spinach leaves
1 green pepper, diced
Tamari sauce and sherry

1. Stir-fry the onions, garlic, rosemary, and sesame seeds in oil, until the onions start to brown.
2. Stir in the hard vegetables (carrots, broccoli, cauliflower). Put the cover on the pan and cook until the vagetables are about half-done, about 6 minutes. Add tamari sauce and sherry to keep everything from sticking.
3. Add the mushrooms. Stir and cook about 4 minutes.
4. Add the spinach leaves and green pepper. As soon as these are just warm, slightly wilted, serve the stir-fry.

Yield: Serves 4

Ratatouille

A French eggplant and zucchini casserole. You stir-fry the vegetables in two halves, then mix them together and bake. Serve ratatouille with millet soufflé, a tossed salad, and red wine for an elegant meal. To make it heartier, bake it with a thick layer of Cheddar or ricotta cheese on top. Then serve it with baked potatoes.

First half:
    2 tablespoons olive oil
    1 eggplant, unpeeled and cut into cubes
    3 medium zucchini, quartered and cut into 1-inch lengths
    1 1/2 teaspoons sea salt
    Freshly ground black pepper
Second half:
    2 tablespoons olive oil
    2 green peppers, coarsely chopped
    4 or more cloves garlic, mashed
    1 bay leaf, chopped together with the garlic to make a fine
        paste
    6 to 8 fresh tomatoes, cut in 1-inch cubes
    1/4 cup finely chopped fresh parsley
    1 tablespoon minced fresh basil or 1 teaspoon dried basil
    1/2 teaspoon dried thyme
    Salt and pepper

1. Heat 2 tablespoons of olive oil in a large skillet, and in it stir-fry the eggplant and zucchini for about 5 minutes. Add salt and pepper.
2. In another skillet, heat 2 more tablespoons of oil, and add the onions and green peppers. Add the garlic-bay leaf paste. Then stir in the tomatoes, and simmer 10 minutes, stirring occasionally. Stir in the parsley, thyme, and basil.
3. Add the eggplant and zucchini to the tomato mixture. Taste.
4. Spoon the mixture into a baking dish, cover, and bake in a 350 degrees F oven for about 30 minutes or until the vegetables are tender.

Variation:
—Add coarsely chopped walnuts.

Yield: Serves 6

Mattar Paneer

A mild curry dish. Serve it hot as a main dish with bright yellow cashew rice. Save a few spoonfuls for filling an omelette.

Butter
2 small onions, finely chopped
2 cups green peas, fresh or frozen
2 teaspoons homemade curry powder
2 to 3 tablespoons finely minced fresh mint leaves or 1
  teaspoon dried mint
2 cooked potatoes, diced with their skins on, or 3 to 4 cooked
  parsnips, diced
2 cups cottage cheese

1. Steam the peas until they're bright green.
2. Stir-fry the onion in butter until it's translucent. Fry in the curry powder. Then mix in the cooked peas and mint.
3. Add the potatoes or parsnips, and cook until they're warm.
4. Remove the pan from the heat, cool it down a bit, then stir in the cottage cheese.
5. Return the pan to the heat to warm it.

Yield: Serves 4

Colache

A bright red, yellow, and green late-summer stir-fry. Serve it for lunch with homemade bread and Cheddar cheese.

Butter
1 medium onion, chopped
2 green or red bell peppers, diced
2 medium zucchini, sliced
2 yellow summer squash, sliced
4 ears fresh sweet corn
1 large tomato, diced
Salt and pepper

1. Stir-fry the onions and peppers in butter until they're limp and glazed.
2. Add the zucchini and yellow squash. Stir-fry until they're tender, about 7 to 8 minutes.
3. Cut the corn kernels from the cob, and add along with the tomato. Cook for 5 minutes or until the corn is tender.
4. Season with sea salt and freshly ground black pepper.

Yield: Serves 4

Stir-Fry Vegetable Chart

Hard vegetables
12 to 15 minutes

Green peppers
Green beans
Celery
Carrots
Broccoli
Cabbage
Cauliflower
Kale
Bok choy
Green tomatoes
Potatoes
Plantains

Medium vegetables
8 to 10 minutes

Asparagus
Mushrooms
Snow peas
Green peas
Zucchini
Yellow summer
   squash
Eggplant
Day lily buds
Radishes
Corn
Red tomatoes

Soft vegetables
3 to 4 minutes

Spinach
Chinese cabbage
Beet greens
Swiss chard
Fresh basil
Fresh parsley
Scallions
Sprouts
Green peppers

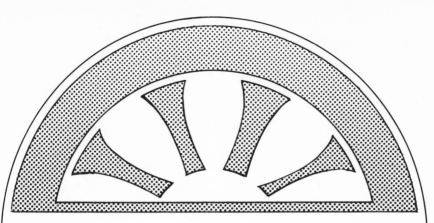

Soups

The advantage of writing my own cookbook is that I can be as pig-headed as I want. And about soup I am very pig-headed: there is one soup. Everything else is just fritzing around. Soup is made of all the vegetables you have available—the more the better. It starts with a tomato base, and is flavored with herbs. It steams with red wine. When you take the lid off the pot, soup fills the room. And it warms you when you eat it.

Some people would call my soup stew. It's true—soup is thick. But this is exactly as it should be. Soup is food, not water. You could live on soup.

SOUP—DETAILED INSTRUCTIONS

Soup is a puttering affair. You assemble the ingredients gradually, cook them over a long period of time, sample, add, and cook some more. The method is important. This recipe tells you how to make the soup base, and how to cook vegetables, grains, and beans in it. Some suggested vegetables and the times at which you add them to the soup are noted in the instructions as you go along. Don't hold yourself back when adding extra ingredients. This recipe makes one warming, steaming potful of soup, enough for six to eight people.

> 1/2 to 1 cup dried beans (1 1/2 to 3 cups cooked beans)
> 1/2 cup uncooked grain (1 cup cooked grain)
> 4 medium onions, chopped
> 2 green peppers, chopped
> 3 or more cloves garlic, mashed
> 1 teaspoon dried basil
> 1 teaspoon dried parsley
> 1 quart home-canned tomatoes, or 6 to 8 fist-sized fresh tomatoes
> Freshly ground black pepper
> 1 teaspoon sea salt, plus more to taste
> Red wine
> Vegetables, all types and plenty of them

1. On the night before you want soup, if you don't have grains or beans already cooked up, start soaking them. Then cook them on the day you're going to make soup. (See the Cooked Grains and Beans chapter for directions.)

2. On the day you want soup—well before you're planning on eating it—get out a big cast iron pot with a lid, or your biggest heavy pot with a cover. (Cooking soup in cast iron is a good idea for more than esthetics: some of the iron from the pot dissolves in the soup, and the iron is available to your body.) Pour a little unrefined oil into the pot, and stir-fry the onions, green peppers, and garlic. Add the basil, parsley, and any other dried herbs you'd like to use. Also fry the spices now. I like using a pinch of

cinnamon or ground allspice in my soups. Fry the herbs and spices in with the onions, stirring all the time.

3. Stir in 1 quart of home-canned tomatoes, juice and all, breaking up the tomatoes with a big wooden spoon. If you're using fresh tomatoes, chop up about 6 to 8 medium-sized ones, and cook them in the onion mixture over low heat so they juice. (If you wish, you can peel fresh tomatoes before you add them. I wouldn't do it, however. Tomato skins add texture to soup.)

4. Grind in lots of black pepper. Add a bay leaf if you're using one. Also stir in any nuts you're using and maybe a fistful of raisins to take the bite out of the tomatoes. (A grated carrot will accomplish the same mellowing trick.) Add 1 teaspoon of sea salt, or 2 teaspoons if you're using fresh tomatoes. (Canned tomatoes already have some salt in them.)

5. Add a nice pour of hearty red wine. Wine gives soup extra fragrance as it cooks, and a richer taste.

6. Cover the pot and begin to simmer the soup. Stir it every now and then, and if it starts getting too thick, stir in a little water, vegetable water, or the water you've cooked the grains and beans in.

7. Start adding vegetables. In general, when cutting vegetables, try to keep all vegetable pieces about the same size. If you're going to eat soup from big bowls, it's fine to leave the vegetables in big pieces. But if you're going to eat from smaller bowls, it's a lot nicer to have smaller vegetable chunks.

You add long-cooking vegetables first—carrots, beets, turnips, potatoes, parsnips, sweet potatoes. Simmer the soup about 30 minutes, until the vegetables are partially cooked and still nicely firm.

8. Add all the medium-cooking vegetables you're using—corn, green and yellow beans, broccoli, cauliflower, okra. Cook about 20 minutes.

9. Add your cooked grains and beans from step 1, along with any extra water you've cooked them in. The water has a lot of flavor, and also contains some of the water-soluble vitamins of the grains and beans. Continue cooking until the grains and beans are heated through.

10. Add the short-cooking vegetables—cabbage, kale, peas, snow peas, summer squash. Dice or shred cabbage, but leave it in nice-sized lumps. You want to be able to identify it. Cook a few more minutes, so the vegetables are tender, but still crisp.

11. Sample soup. Tasting is essential. You will almost always want to reseason it—a pinch more salt, a few grinds more of black pepper, a dash more wine, or a squirt of fresh lemon juice or red wine vinegar for lightness. If the soup is too thick, add more vegetable water.

12. A few minutes before eating the soup, break the delicate greens onto the top of the simmering soup—spinach, Swiss chard, beet greens, fresh basil, Chinese cabbage. Be sure to break the greens into small pieces, or they will cook up into long strands which are difficult to swallow. Put the lid back on the pot and continue simmering. The greens on top will steam in the vapors from the soup and will keep their color. Mix them into the soup when they're cooked.

13. Right before you want to eat, snip fresh basil, parsley, scallions, or chives into the soup for their bright color and freshness.

14. And now you have a potful of soup. Soup by itself is a feast. Or top it with grated Cheddar cheese, a dollop of yoghurt, or ricotta cheese. Sprinkle it with more finely minced fresh herbs. Or ladle soup over a mound of cottage cheese in a bowl. The warm soup steeps down through the cheese curds. If you're making lunch for someone who's working, pack hot soup in a thermos. When your friend opens the soup, it's almost as if you were there too.

Cashew Chili

Exciting, a little hot, with lots of surprises—especially raisins and cashews. Serve with grated colby or Monterey jack cheese, and with steamy warm cornbread or cooked brown rice.

Chili powder is a blend of spices. Chile powder is dried red chile peppers ground up. For information on ordering freshly ground dried chile powder, see the recipe for red chile sauce.

> 2 to 3 cups cooked kidney or pinto beans (1 cup dry)
> 4 medium onions, chopped
> 2 green peppers, chopped
> 2 stalks celery, finely chopped
> 3 or more cloves garlic, mashed
> 1 teaspoon dried basil
> 1 teaspoon oregano
> 1 tablespoon chili or 1/2 teaspoon chile powder
> 1 teaspoon ground cumin
> 1 quart home-canned tomatoes
> Freshly ground black pepper
> 1 bay leaf
> 1/2 to 1 cup cashews
> 1 handful raisins or 1 tablespoon molasses
> 1 teaspoon sea salt
> 1/4 cup (more or less) red wine vinegar or cider vinegar

Follow the detailed soup instructions. Stir-fry the celery in with the onions and peppers. Add the vinegar a little at a time, tasting between additions, when the chili is almost ready to serve.

Variations:
—You can make chili as hot as you like by adding more chili or chile powder. Mild chili is a more subtle pleasure.
—Add 3 or 4 carrots or parsnips, diced, for sweet tastes and a different texture.
—Add snap beans for a lighter, greener chili.
—A dash or 2 of sherry is good in chili; and believe it or not, beer is the most delicious liquid in which to cook beans or to thin chili.

Yield: Serves 6 to 8

Curried Lentil Soup

A spicy fast soup, especially good for hot days. Ladle it over cooked brown rice, and serve yoghurt and chopped bananas to mix in.

    2 to 3 cups cooked lentils (1 cup dry)
    4 to 6 medium onions, chopped
    2 to 4 green peppers, chopped
    3 cloves garlic, mashed
    Curry spices:
        1 teaspoon ground turmeric
        1 teaspoon ground cumin
        1 teaspoon ground coriander
        3 whole cloves, ground
        1 teaspoon chili or chile powder
        2 teaspoons minced fresh ginger (1/2 teaspoon dry ginger)
    1 quart home-canned tomatoes
    1 handful raisins
    1 teaspoon sea salt
    Extra water to thin soup
    Juice 1 lemon

Follow the detailed soup instructions. Grind the curry spices in a mortar and pestle or in your grain mill. Mix them together and add them to the onions after the onions are fried. Fry the spices quickly, stirring so they don't stick and burn. If they do start to stick, add a bit more oil. Add the lemon juice right before serving the soup.

Variations:
—For more curry spices you might add, see the Index.
—Mix chopped fresh coriander leaves into the cooked soup.

Yield: Serves 6 to 8

Green Pea Barley Soup

This soup is a classic. Marjoram, especially fresh marjoram, is the best herb with green peas. Bleu cheese crumbled over green pea barley soup is delicious.

    2 to 3 cups cooked soybeans (1/2 to 1 cup dry)
    1 1/2 to 2 cups cooked barley (1/2 cup uncooked)
    4 medium onions, chopped
    3 cloves garlic, mashed
    2 teaspoons dried or fresh marjoram
    1 quart home-canned tomatoes
    1 bay leaf
    1 teaspoon sea salt
    Red wine
    2 big carrots, diced into cubes the size of green peas
    3 stalks celery, diced
    2 cups green peas, fresh or frozen
    Handful chopped fresh parsley

Follow the detailed soup instructions.

Yield: Serves 6 to 8

Black Bean Soup

No cookbook would be complete without this recipe. Serve garnished with slices of lemon and hard-cooked eggs, or with strips of pimento.

2 cups dry black beans
2 teaspoons sea salt
Peanut oil
4 medium onions, finely chopped
1 green pepper, finely chopped
3 cloves garlic, mashed
1 teaspoon cumin seed
1 teaspoon oregano
1/2 teaspoon dry mustard
1/4 quart home-canned tomatoes, or 2 fresh tomatoes
Juice 1/2 lemon

Follow the detailed soup instructions. Cook the black beans in lots of extra water with the 2 teaspoons sea salt. After you add the beans and cooking water to the main bulk of the soup, mash some of the beans up so the whole soup is very thick. Add the lemon juice just before serving.

Variations:
—Add chopped green olives or chopped pimentos.

Yield: Serves 6 to 8

Bright Dill Borscht

Sweet and sour with raisins and cider vinegar, bright orange and purple with carrots and beets. Serve with ricotta cheese or yoghurt. It's especially good cold the second day.

    4 medium onions, chopped
    Handful chopped fresh dill weed, or
        1 tablespoon dried dill weed
    1 quart home-canned tomatoes
    Freshly ground black pepper
    2 handfuls raisins
    1 teaspoon sea salt
    8 beets with their greens, all sliced
    4 carrots, sliced
    1/4 cup cider vinegar

Follow the detailed soup instructions. Add the vinegar along with the carrots and beets. Save the beet greens until the end. Simmer them on top of the soup, then mix them in.

Yield: Serves 6 to 8

Dumbfounding Caraway Borscht

A grated cabbage and beet soup, flavored with caraway seeds, orange juice, and cloves. Sour cream makes it smooth. Dollop an extra bit of sour cream on top of each bowlful when you serve it.

4 medium onions, grated
1 tablespoon butter
1 quart home-canned tomatoes
1/2 head cabbage, grated
6 to 8 fresh beets, grated
2 whole cloves, ground
1 tablespoon caraway seeds
2 tablespoons cider vinegar
Grated rind and juice of 1 orange
2 teaspoons sea salt
1 cup sour cream

1. Grate the onions. People will be crying 4 rooms away when you do this. Sauté 2 of the grated onions in butter.
2. Add the tomatoes, mashing them up with a wooden spoon so they're smooth.
3. Add the other 2 grated onions, the cabbage, and the beets. Stir everything well.
4. Add the cloves, caraway seeds, vinegar, orange rind and juice, and salt.
5. Cover the pot and simmer, stirring every now and then, for about 1 hour.
6. Taste. If all the flavors do not stand out nicely, try adding more vinegar or salt.
7. Take the soup off the stove. Ladle about 2 cups out of the pot, and mix it with the sour cream. Then mix that back into the main bulk of the soup.

Yield: Serves 6 to 8

Extravagant Minestrone

Cooked chick peas, squiggles of noodles, and the taste of cinnamon make this a festive soup. Sprinkle bowls with coarsely grated Parmesan cheese.

    1 to 2 cups cooked chick peas (1/2 cup dry)
    3 cups cooked whole wheat noodles (1 cup uncooked)
    4 medium onions, chopped
    3 cloves garlic, mashed
    1 teaspoon dried basil
    1 teaspoon oregano
    A few pinches ground cinnamon
    1 quart home-canned tomatoes
    Freshly ground black pepper
    1 handful raisins
    1 teaspoon sea salt
    Lots of red wine
    2 or 3 big carrots, diced
    1 small turnip, diced
    2 cups green snap beans
    2 cups green peas
    1/4 head cabbage
    Small handful chopped fresh basil
    Dash red wine vinegar

Follow the detailed soup instructions. Add the noodles right at the end of the cooking period, and cook more just to heat them. Of all noodles, whole wheat elbow macaroni keeps its shape the best.

Yield: Serves 6 to 8

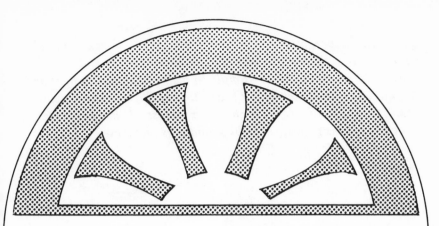

Omelettes, Crêpes, Etc.

Omelettes, crêpes, quiches, and pizza are dishes you can impress your friends with, for although they're cosmopolitan and considered gourmet, they're simple to make. Each dish is light and elegant—good for lunch or for a late dinner. (Pizza is the heaviest of the four.) Furthermore, each dish is almost a balanced meal, since it contains grains, vegetables, and eggs or cheese.

OMELETTES

An omelette is a thick egg pancake, a very simple food which is tender and delicious. Omelettes are good for breakfast, for lunch, and with salad, bread, and wine for dinner.

A well-seasoned omelette pan helps you make better omelettes. Omelettes slide out easily, without sticking. I recommend getting a real French omelette pan, which has sloping sides. Otherwise, reserve a good-sized frying pan, about eight to nine inches in diameter, especially for omelettes.

Wash the pan well. Fill it almost to the top with cooking oil and place it on a slow heat, just warm enough to allow the oil to work its way into the pores of the metal. Keep the panful of oil at this temperature for at least three hours. Remove it from the heat and let the oil stand in the pan overnight. In the morning pour off the oil and save it in a jar for future cleanings of the pan. Wipe the pan dry with a soft cloth. Now the pan is ready to cook omelettes: it will be a little oily, not greasy.

Once it's seasoned, try not to wash the pan in water again. Each time you make an omelette, as soon as you've finished, sprinkle the pan with salt for a mild abrasive, then wipe it clean with a piece of paper or a soft cloth. If your pan does get washed or 'deseasoned', however, follow the initial seasoning procedure to season it again.

Plain Omelette

A two or three egg omelette serves one person, or can be cut in half for two people. There are many omelette-making techniques. The one used here is fail-safe.

>   1 scant tablespoon butter
>   2 or 3 fresh eggs

1. Put the omelette pan on the stove over slow heat and add the butter.
2. While the butter is melting, crack the eggs into a bowl and beat them briskly with a fork or a whisk. Beat about 20 to 30 times so they're well-beaten.
3. Turn up the heat under the pan, and as soon as the butter starts to foam, pour the beaten eggs directly into the pan. (I use butter for omelettes rather than oil because of this foaming. It tells exactly how hot the pan is. With oil there is no such indication, and the pan may get very hot and scorch the eggs.)
4. Let the eggs cook for a minute or 2.
5. When the eggs begin to set, lift up 1 edge of the cooked pancake with a spatula. Tilt the pan so some of the uncooked egg from the top runs under. Lift up the other edges of the omelette and tilt the pan until most of the liquid egg is under the cooked part.
6. Cook a minute or 2 longer, or until the eggs are as done as you like them. I like omelettes evenly cooked the whole way through. You can also cook them so the eggs are well-done on the outside and soft on the inside.
7. Fold the omelette in half and lift it with the spatula onto a serving plate.

Variations:
—For a fresh herb omelette, whisk finely minced fresh herbs in with the eggs when you beat them.
—Puffy omelette—Separate the egg whites and yolks. Whisk the whites in a separate bowl until they're stiff. Beat the egg yolks, then fold the whites into the yolks. Be gentle so the mixture stays foamy. Cook the omelette just as you'd cook a regular omelette, but a little more slowly.

Yield: Serves 1 or 2

Omelette Fillings

Make fillings before you start cooking the eggs. I put hot stir-fried vegetables on the omelette after step five above, when all the uncooked egg has been tilted to the bottom of the pan. Then I let the eggs and vegetables cook for a minute or two, fold the omelette in half, and serve it. If I'm making a cheese omelette, I grate hard cheeses and sprinkle them over the partially cooked eggs after step five, or over the vegetables if I've used them too. Then I pop the omelette under the broiler until the cheese melts, then fold it. If I'm using ricotta or cottage cheese, I smooth them over the partially cooked eggs or the vegetables, and immediately cover the omelette pan with a plate so the steam from the cooking eggs can warm the cheese through. Then I take off the plate, fold the omelette, and serve the omelette on the cooking plate while it's still warm. Following are some fillings I enjoy.

Stir-fried shallots and fresh herbs

Watercress and homemade croutons; served with sour cream

Stir-fried mushrooms, freshly grated nutmeg, and grated Swiss cheese

California omelette—Fresh tomato slices, avocado slices, and grated Monterey jack cheese; served with sourdough bread or with refried beans

Omelette Louis—Cottage cheese, mixed with nutmeg and chopped chives; Swiss cheese melted over that

Mexican omelette—Fill an omelette with lots of guacamole; serve with sour cream

Spanish omelette—Stir-fried onions, green peppers, and potatoes; covered with warm tomato sauce

Mushroom fu-yung omelette—Stir-fried mushrooms, green peppers, scallions, and sprouts, mixed with a little tamari sauce

Italian omelette—Stir-fried tomato slices with garlic, pine nuts or walnuts, basil, and black pepper; then a little grated Parmesan cheese

Curry omelette—Fill an omelette with leftover curry; mix a little grated coconut into the eggs for unusual texture

CRÊPES

Crêpes are fairly large, thin pancakes. They can be rolled around fillings and served as you make them, like omelettes. They can be filled, arranged in a baking dish, covered with a creamy sauce, and heated in the oven until you're ready to eat. Or they can be stacked flat with layers of fillings between them, covered with a sauce, baked, then cut into slices.

A French crêpe pan is good for cooking crêpes, but any medium-size cast iron skillet works as well. I usually cook crêpes in a seven or eight inch cast iron pan.

Try to make crêpe batter at least two hours before you want to cook the crêpes: if the batter can rest, it's easier to cook. People often mix up crêpe batter the night before they want to make them.

Crêpes can be made from varying proportions of flour, milk, and eggs. I like this recipe because it always works: the crêpes hold together and don't stick. Buckwheat flour makes thin, delicate crêpes because it's so finely ground. Even many traditional French crêpes were made with buckwheat flour. Whole wheat pastry flour makes a thicker crêpe, but one which has the buttery whole wheat taste.

> 1 1/2 cups buckwheat flour or 2 cups whole wheat pastry flour
> 1/2 teaspoon sea salt
> 4 eggs
> 2 cups milk

1. With a wooden spoon stir the flour and salt together in a mixing bowl.
2. Add the eggs 1 at a time, and stir them into the batter.
3. Add the milk little by little, stirring it in well after each addition so the batter doesn't lump. After you've added all the milk, keep stirring until the batter is smooth. (If it lumps a little, either ignore the lumps or remove them with a small spoon.)
4. When you're ready to start cooking crêpes, heat your crêpe pan over medium heat, add a little butter, and tip the pan around until the butter coats the bottom.

5. When the butter starts sizzling, stir up the crêpe batter, and ladle a small amount into the pan. Swirl it around until the batter fills the pan. (I ladle batter into my pan with a 1/4 cup measuring cup so the crêpes will all be the same size.)

6. Cook the crêpe until it looks firm and flippable, then flip it with a spatula and cook it for just a few seconds on the other side. It should be lightly browned on both sides. Don't be discouraged if the first crêpe in each batch you make sticks or falls apart. Cooking the first crêpe seasons the pan so the rest will come out easily.

7. Continue cooking crêpes until the batter is used up. Butter the pan lightly between crêpes. Either fill the crêpes as you make them, or stack them on a plate and fill them when you're all through.

Yield: 14 to 16 7 or 8 inch crêpes

Fruit Filled Crêpes

Fruit-filled crêpes are special for breakfast or dessert. I fill crêpes with fruit salad, then pour lots of honey yoghurt dressing over them.

Fruit-filled crêpes are especially good if you brush each crêpe as you make it with a little orange liqueur, such as Cointreau or Grand Marnier, then stack the crêpes on top of each other. The liqueur soaks into the crêpes and adds a delicious flavor. Try mixing a little liqueur into the yoghurt dressing.

Fruit crêpes can also be baked to warm them. For dessert I like crêpes filled with sliced bananas, walnuts, cottage cheese, cinnamon, and raisins; then covered with a dressing of melted butter mixed with a little honey and lemon juice, and baked for twenty to thirty minutes in a 350 degrees F oven. Try serving ice cream over hot fruit crêpes.

Vegetable Filled Crêpes

Vegetable crêpes are a main dish. I make stir-fried vegetables and mix them with a seasoned white sauce, grated cheese, or cottage cheese. I spoon as much filling as I can fit into each crêpe, since crêpes are much more luscious if they're filled to plumpness. I roll it up, and arrange all the crêpes in a buttered baking dish. Finally I cover the crêpes with a generous amount of white sauce, and bake them about twenty to thirty minutes in a 350 degrees F oven to warm them. The white sauce is good if it's seasoned with the herbs used in the stir-fried vegetables. But really almost everything goes.

Following is a list of several favorite fillings.

Stir-fried broccoli or cauliflower, mixed with Cheddar cheese; baked with a Cheddar cheese white sauce

Sesame cauliflower crêpes—Stir-fried cauliflower and onions, mixed with sesame seeds and tahini; baked with a white sauce flavored with tahini and yoghurt; sprinkle with sesame seeds; serve with orange and onion salad

Cashew mushroom crêpes—Stir-fried mushrooms and onions, mixed mixed with whole cashews; baked with a white sauce flavored with cashew butter

Stir-fried asparagus and onions, mixed with ricotta cheese; baked with a nutmeg white sauce

Stir-fried spinach, mushrooms, and onions, mixed with grated Swiss cheese; baked with a Swiss cheese and nutmeg white sauce

Spring vegetable crêpes—Sweet spring parsnips stir-fried in butter with onions and asparagus, mixed with a sherry white sauce; baked with more sherry white sauce

Ratatouille crêpes—Ratatouille in crepes; baked with a Parmesan cheese white sauce

Colache crêpes—Colache mixed with grated Cheddar cheese; baked with a Cheddar cheese white sauce

Crêpe Manicotti With 2 Sauces

This is the most gourmet of all the main dishes I make. Roll a cheese and cinnamon filling in crêpes, then bake them with a tomato sauce below and a red wine and nutmeg white sauce above. Manicotti is rich and shapely. Save it for special dinners, when you want to do a lot of cooking.

14 to 16 crêpes
Filling:
    1 pound ricotta cheese
    1 pound mozzarella cheese, grated
    A good-sized lump of Parmesan cheese, coarsely grated
    Lots of raisins
    2 eggs
    2 teaspoons cinnamon
    1/2 teaspoon sea salt
    Lots of fresh parsley and scallions, finely minced
    Red wine
2 cups long-simmered tomato sauce with cinnamon and red wine added (See pages 210-211)
1 quart basic whole wheat white sauce with nutmeg and red wine added (See pages 214-215)

1. Make the crêpes.
2. Mix together the ingredients of the filling. Add red wine until the mixture has a firm but creamy consistency.
3. Roll a good-sized helping of filling inside each crêpe.
4. Spread the bottom of a baking dish with the tomato sauce. In it arrange the crêpes. Push them against each other so they will stay rolled. Pour the white sauce over everything. Sprinkle it with finely minced fresh parsley.
5. Bake for 30 to 40 minutes in a 350 degrees F oven, then turn the oven off and leave the manicotti in it for about 1/2 hour before serving so the flavors can ripen.

Yield: Serves 6

QUICHES & VEGETABLE PIES

Pie Crust

To make a good pie crust, you need a fat which is partially solid at room temperature. As far as I can see, butter is the only option. Not only is a butter crust delicious, but the alternatives—margarine or hydrogenated vegetable oils—are highly processed and artificial foods. When you make pie dough, you cut the butter into pea-sized pieces. Part of each piece melts to coat the particles of flour and keep the pie crust tender by preventing gluten from forming. The rest of each piece melts when the crust bakes, forming pockets in the dough which are filled with steam and make the crust flaky. Liquid oils cannot melt to form pockets, so oil crusts are doomed to be mealy.

Use whole wheat pastry flour to make pie crusts. It comes from soft wheat berries, which have less gluten than hard wheat, so it makes your crust tender, rather than tough like bread dough.

I always make two pie crusts at once: if it's worth making one quiche or vegetable pie, it's worth making two.

> 2 cups whole wheat pastry flour
> 1 teaspoon sea salt
> 1/2 cup butter
> 1/4 cup (more or less) cold water

1. Mix the flour and salt together in a medium-size mixing bowl.
2. Add the butter, and using a pastry blender or 2 forks, cut the butter into the flour until the largest pieces of butter are the size of small peas.
3. Sprinkle a small amount of water over some of the mixture and toss it lightly with a fork. Push the damp part to one side. Then add water to another portion and toss until all the dough is dampened. (You may not use the full 1/4 cup water.) Toss the dough gently during this process to work up some gluten to hold the crust together, but not so much gluten that the dough will be tough.
4. Stir the mixture with firm strokes of the fork until the dough

forms a ball that does not cling to the sides of the bowl.

5. Divide the dough in half. With the following procedure, roll out one half, then the other.

6. Pick up the dough in your hands and press it together between cupped palms, turning the dough 4 times. Do not knead it. Press the dough into a flattened ball, building up the edges higher than the center and pinching the edges together if the dough cracks.

7. Lightly flour a counter and your rolling pin. Brush aside any extra flour, leaving only a thin film.

8. Roll lightly, working from the center to the outside, picking the dough up and turning it occasionally so it doesn't stick. Flour the counter more if you need to. Roll until the diameter of the dough is 1 inch larger than that of your inverted pie pan. If the dough comes to pieces as you roll it, moisten the edges of the pieces and stick them back together.

9. Roll the dough carefully over the rolling pin, loosening it from the counter with a knife if it sticks, and lift it into the ungreased pie pan. Let the weight of the pastry ease it into place without stretching.

10. Trim the pastry, leaving about 1/2 inch overhang. Turn the edge under all the way around.

11. For a nice-looking crust, flute the rim: place your right thumb against the outside of the fold; then place the left thumb and index finger on the inside edge on either side of the right thumb; press in firmly with your right thumb. Travel around the edge of the crust doing this.

12. In about 4 places, tuck the edge of the crust under the pie pan and press it there. This is to hold the crust and keep it from shrinking too much.

You now have unbaked pie shells, ready for filling.

Variations:
—Mix minced fresh dill or dried dill weed in with the salt and flour.
—Use white wine or buttermilk for the liquid.
—Grate in some Cheddar cheese for a cheese crust.
—A few tablespoons of poppy seeds give a crunchier crust.

Yield: 2 9-inch pie crusts

Quiche Fillings

You make quiches in three layers. First you put a layer of stir-fried vegetables with herbs on the bottom of your unbaked pie crust. On top of the vegetables you spread a layer of grated cheese—about one cup or enough to cover the vegetables nicely. It's best to use strong cheeses, so you can taste them. For the third layer you make a custard mixture, which you pour over the cheese. During baking it puffs up, a golden brown bubble. Here is a recipe for the custard for one quiche.

    2 eggs, lightly beaten
    1 cup milk
    1/2 teaspoon salt

Mix all the ingredients together, and beat with a fork or a wire whisk until they're well-blended. (To vary the custard mixture, whisk in some of the herbs and seasonings you used in the stir-fried vegetables.)

Bake the quiche in a 350 degrees F oven for about forty to fifty minutes, or until the top is golden and firm. I usually turn off the oven after forty minutes and allow the quiche to finish cooking slowly. I leave it in the oven until I'm ready to serve it.

Quiches can be served warm from the oven, or at room temperature the next day. Served with salad and wine, a quiche is a light and satisfying meal.

Following are suggestions for quiche vegetables, cheeses, and custard seasonings.

Onion quiche—Stir-fried onions, Cheddar cheese, and thyme or caraway seeds in the custard

Parmesan quiche—Onions and green peppers, stir-fried in olive oil, Parmesan cheese, and pine nuts in the custard

Zucchini quiche—Stir-fried zucchini slices (Add slices of yellow summer squash for color.) with rosemary, Cheddar cheese, and more rosemary in the custard

Classic quiche—Stir-fried spinach and mushrooms, Swiss cheese, and nutmeg in the custard

Dilly bean quiche—Stir-fried green beans and onions with fresh dill, Swiss cheese, and more fresh dill in the custard

Vegetable Pie Fillings

To make vegetable pies, I make well-seasoned stir-fried vegetables, enough to fill the pie shell slightly mounded. I make a sauce for them, mix a little white sauce with the vegetables, put the mixture in the shell, and pour the rest of the sauce over the top. I bake the pie in a 350 degrees F oven for about forty to fifty minutes, or until the crust is browned and the filling is warm and bubbly. (See pages 214-215 for a whole wheat white sauce recipe.)

Following are several of my favorite vegetable pie fillings.

Homemade sauerkraut stir-fried with lots of onions, mushrooms, caraway seeds, and paprika, then mixed with white sauce. Pour white sauce over the top, dust well with paprika, and bake.

Russian peasant pie—Onions, sliced carrots, sliced turnips, and red cabbage, all stir-fried with dill seed and basil. Mix with white sauce sauce, pour more white sauce over the top, and bake.

Parsnip pie—Onions and parsnips stir-fried with minced fresh ginger, roasted peanuts, and a little sherry. Mix in peanut butter onion sauce, smooth more sauce over the top of the pie, and bake.

Deep dish ricotta spinach pie—Ricotta cheese mixed with stir-fried mushrooms and spinach. Mix in 2 eggs, and season with salt, pepper, nutmeg, and a few fresh scallions, finely chopped. Cover with grated Parmesan cheese, and bake.

PIZZA

With a whole wheat crust and lots of fresh vegetables on top, pizza is a delicious and nutritious food. I like it for dinner with a big salad, red wine, and ice cream for dessert. Pizza is perfect to make when two people are cooking: one person makes the crust, and the other makes the fillings.

Pizza Crust

For pizza crust I make grainy bread dough. Half a recipeful of dough (1 1/4 cups liquid) will make crust for one rectangular pizza on a cookie sheet, one round pizza in a pizza pan, or two small pizzas in pie plates. A whole recipeful of dough (2 1/2 cups liquid) will make crust for two big pizzas or four little ones. I usually make make a whole recipeful of dough, and use what I have left over to make a loaf of bread or a few rolls.

1. Make standard grainy bread dough. (See the Bread Is Basic chapter for a recipe and instructions.)
2. After the dough has risen a second time, punch it down. Lightly oil the pizza pan or pans you're going to use. Cut the dough into pieces, and with a rolling pin roll out each piece to fit a pan. Roll the crust thick or thin, however you prefer. Fit each crust into a pan, press the edges of the crust up onto the sides of the pan to make a little ridge, and prick the crust all over with a fork so it won't puff up when it bakes.
3. Put the crusts immediately into a 425 degrees F oven, and bake them for 10 to 15 minutes. I've found this pre-baking is necessary for the crust and pizza filling to both get done at the same time.

Variations:
—Use olive oil in the dough, and add 2 teaspoons dried marjoram.
—Add a little freshly ground black pepper to the dough.
—Add grated Cheddar or Parmesan cheese to the dough.
—For my special raisin bread pizza, I add several handfuls of raisins to the dough. Then I put cinnamon in the tomato sauce.

Pizza Fillings

Tomato sauce, long-simmered or just-cooked (See pages 209-211.)
Lots of Mozzarella cheese, grated
Parmesan cheese, grated
Stir-fried vegetables (alone or in any combination):
    Zucchini and yellow summer squash, sliced
    Eggplant, sliced
    Mushrooms, cut in thick slices
    Green pepper rings
    Onion rings
    Broccoli or cauliflower, slices and flowerettes

1. Make the tomato sauce, grate the cheeses, and stir-fry the vegetables you've selected in olive oil. Don't overcook the vegetables.
2. After the pizza crust has pre-baked 10 to 15 minutes, take it out of the oven, and spread a layer of tomato sauce over it. Arrange the stir-fried vegetables in the sauce. This can be done in ornate patterns with a few vegetables, or you can mound lots of vegetables on the pizza so each slice is a gorgeous heap.
3. Bake this partial pizza 15 minutes more.
4. Take it out of the oven, cover the pizza with a thick layer of grated mozzarella cheese, and sprinkle it with Parmesan cheese.
5. Pop the pizza back in the oven, and bake it 10 minutes or until the cheese is bubbly. Serve the pizza hot from the oven.

Variations:
—Stir-fry the vegetables in olive oil with mashed garlic and herbs such as oregano, basil, and marjoram.
—Add chopped black olives to the vegetables.
—Add cooked chick peas to the vegetables.
—Prepare eggplant slices as for eggplant parmigiane (See Index).
—Add cinnamon to the tomato sauce for raisin bread pizza.

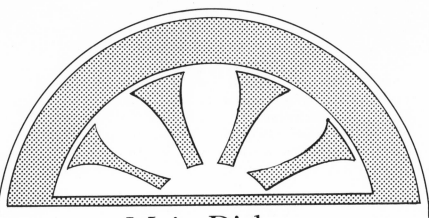

Main Dishes

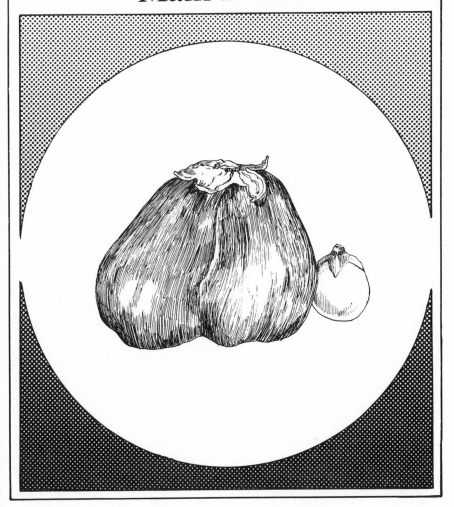

Dinner is a time to talk, to relax with friends, and a time to appreciate good food. I feel that cooking dinner is as important as eating. I like to make an interesting main dish, one that takes time to prepare, so friends can help cook. We sip wine as we chop vegetables and grate cheese. We toss a big salad, carry fresh bread, butter, and cheese to the dinner table, and pour glasses full of red wine. Finally we light a candle, and sit down to eat. Dinner is a sacred time of the day, and deserves special food to go with it.

PASTA DISHES

Whole wheat pasta in several different shapes is available in natural foods stores. You can also find green spinach pasta, and pasta made from other whole grains, such as rice and corn, in larger stores. See the Index to make your own pasta and for directions for cooking pasta.

The simplest pasta dishes are made by cooking pasta and tossing it with a sauce while it's still hot. I think fettuccine, 'little ribbons,' are the best shape to toss. Pasta dishes should always be tossed at the last minute so the pasta and the sauces each keep their clean tastes and textures. Try hot fettuccine tossed with just-cooked tomato sauce, with lots of Parmesan cheese coarsely grated over it. Or try fettuccine tossed with stir-fried zucchini and sesame onion sauce. Or try fettuccine tossed with stir-fried mushrooms and a nutmeg and sherry white sauce.

Arranged pasta dishes are ideal to serve to company. You put a heap of steamed asparagus, broccoli, or cauliflower in the center of a baking dish. Surround it with rings of stir-fried mushrooms and cooked pasta. Cover it all with tomato sauce and mozzarella cheese, then bake it in a 350 degrees F oven for twenty to thirty minutes, or until the cheese is melted and the vegetables are hot. For a special touch, arrange an individual pasta casserole in an au gratin dish for each person. The pasta and vegetables etched in cheese will be very beautiful.

People enjoy slicing through a casserole and finding layers—each with a separate taste, texture, and color. After I bake a layered pasta dish, I turn off the oven and leave the casserole in it to rest for at least half an hour before I serve it. This firms the layers and allows the casserole to reach a temperature good for eating. If I have company I can relax while my casserole is resting, and can serve it when I want to rather than on a rigid schedule.

Green Lasagne

One layer of lasagne is always wide lasagne noodles. The other layers are subject to a lot of creativity. My green lasagne has layers of whole wheat lasagne noodles (Homemade green noodles are the best.), Italian cheeses, spinach, and long-simmered tomato sauce. Cottage cheese is a fair substitute for ricotta if you mix in an egg to firm it up a bit.

I recommend baking green lasagne in pottery, glass, or enamel baking dishes. Naked metal pans, particularly aluminum ones, react with the tomato sauce, and you lose the flavor of the casserole. This recipe fills a nine by thirteen inch baking dish. But you can use any combination of pans. Make a little side dish if you have anything left over.

With lasagne I serve a colorful tossed salad, full of spinach, carrots, fresh tomatoes, hard-cooked eggs, and capers. I like to end lasagne dinners in the living room, with mugs of steaming dark-roast coffee, and fruit, cheese, and nuts to nibble.

Layer A:
  1 quart long-simmered tomato sauce (See pages 210-211)
Layer B:
  1/2 to 1 pound whole wheat lasagne noodles
Layer C:
  1 pound spinach or Swiss chard, cooked
  2 eggs, lightly beaten
  1/4 teaspoon freshly grated nutmeg
Layer D:
  1 pound ricotta cheese
Layer E:
  1 pound mozzarella cheese, grated or sliced
Layer F:
  Parmesan or Romano cheese, grated

1. Make the tomato sauce, cook up the pasta, and prepare the cheeses.
2. Cook the spinach, and mix it with the eggs and nutmeg.
3. Layer the ingredients in a baking dish, starting with tomato sauce on the bottom. Layer in cycles: ABCDEF, ABCDEF until all the ingredients are used up. Try to end with a layer of mozzarella.
4. Bake lasagne in a 350 degrees F oven for 30 to 40 minutes or slightly longer if you started with cold tomato sauce. Baking melts the cheeses and heats the casserole through. Then turn off the oven and leave the lasagne for about 30 minutes, or until you're ready to serve dinner.

Variations:
—Leave out the spinach, and add a layer of stir-fried mushrooms, eggplant, or onion rings.
—Add a layer of seasoned cooked lentils.
—Use a seasoned white sauce in place of the cheeses.
—Try mixing chopped black olives in with the ricotta cheese.

Yield: Serves 6

Funistrada

Funistrada is a casserole with layers of three kinds of noodles, stir-fried zucchini, and a tarragon white sauce. Its origin is unusual.

My father went to a lecture given by a man who had surveyed the food preferences of army personnel. The surveyor had given his sample of army men a questionnaire listing four hundred food items, and the men rated each food as to how much they liked it and how often they ate it. The questionnaire included four phony items to check the validity of the ratings. One phony item, Dad told me, was called 'funistrada.'

As soon as I heard that, I had to invent funistrada. It had to have layers, because of the 'strada.' And it had to be 'funny'—hence the three types of pasta, the curlier the better. (You can make funistrada with one kind of pasta, but it loses its magic.) Then independently my friend Patti and I both decided that funistrada needed a tarragon white sauce. We're excited because funistrada turned out to be good! It's smoothly grainy, and tastes of tarragon, which highlights the zucchini.

I serve funistrada with a big green salad with fresh dill, raisins, and yoghurt tahini dressing.

Layer A:
   1 quart whole wheat white sauce (See pages 214-215)
   1 tablespoon dried or fresh tarragon
   2 teaspoons dried dill weed or 1/4 cup fresh dill weed
   1 teaspoon thyme
   1/2 teaspoon extra sea salt
   1/4 cup red wine
Layer B:
   1/4 pound (about 1 cup) each of any 3 different types of uncooked whole wheat pasta

Layer C:
- 3 or 4 medium onions, sliced in rings
- 2 teaspoons dried tarragon
- 2 or 3 medium zucchini, sliced
- 3 or more big handfuls raisins
- 2 teaspoons sea salt
- Lots of freshly ground black pepper

1. Make the white sauce, adding the extra herbs with the milk, and adding the wine after the sauce has cooked and you've removed it from the heat.

2. Cook up each of the pastas separately. (Or use about 3 cups each of any 3 kinds of cooked pasta you have. Funistrada is a good way to use leftover noodles.)

3. Stir-fry the onions, tarragon, and zucchini in olive oil until the zucchini is tender. Add the raisins, salt, and pepper. Pour off any juice and save it for soup.

4. Start layering in a casserole dish with a thin coating of white sauce on the bottom. Then spread on it all of 1 type of pasta. Cover that with the zucchini and onion mixture. Then proceed layering ABC, ABC. End with a layer of white sauce.

5. Bake funistrada in a 350 degrees F oven for 30 to 40 minutes, then turn off the oven and let the casserole rest for 30 minutes or until you're ready to serve it.

Yield: Serves 6

Sinfully Rich Fettuccine

Butter, ricotta, and Parmesan cheeses tossed with hot fettuccine and cooked sweet young green peas. Serve it with green salad.

2 cups uncooked whole wheat fettuccine (5 cups cooked)
1/4 cup butter, cut in pat-size pieces
1 cup ricotta cheese
1/2 cup freshly grated Parmesan cheese
3/4 cup milk or light cream
2 cups green peas, fresh or frozen
Freshly grated nutmeg
Freshly ground black pepper
2 handfuls chopped fresh parsley

1. Cook the pasta, and drain it. Cook the peas until they're just tender.
2. Get everything else ready. Then get out either a big skillet or a big chafing dish.
3. Heat up the skillet or chafing dish. In it toss the noodles and the butter pats. Simmer a minute.
4. Toss in the ricotta and Parmesan cheeses. Stir in the milk or cream.
5. Now grate nutmeg and grind pepper over the dish. This could be magnificent: move your elbows.
6. Toss in the fresh parsley and serve immediately.

Yield: Serves 4

Mom's Macaroni & Cheese

A special family recipe. This casserole is custardy, moist, and tender. It has a livelier, 'greener' taste than you're used to in macaroni and cheese.

> 1 cup uncooked whole wheat or buckwheat macaroni (or 3 cups of any cooked pasta)
> 1 1/4 cups hot milk
> 3/8 cup dry bread crumbs or 3/4 cup fresh bread crumbs
> 1/2 pound Cheddar cheese, grated
> 1 medium onion, finely chopped
> 1 green pepper, finely chopped
> Lots of fresh parsley or watercress, finely minced
> (3 or 4 scallions, finely minced, optional)
> 1 teaspoon sea salt
> 2 eggs, well-beaten

1. Cook the macaroni until it's tender but still firm. (See the Index for pasta cooking instructions.) Drain it.
2. Pour the hot milk over the bread crumbs and cheese in a big bowl. Add the onion, green pepper, parsley or watercress, scallions, and salt. Stir in the eggs, then mix in the cooked macaroni.
3. Put the mixture in a buttered casserole dish. Sprinkle with paprika.
4. Bake in a 350 degrees F oven for about 30 minutes, or until the casserole is firm and golden-brown.

Variation:
—If you're feeling extravagant, top the casserole with a layer of sliced, stir-fried mushrooms.

Yield: Serves 4

Tante Kathinka's Corn Pudding

This is a simple corny custard. I serve it as part of a hot vegetable plate, usually with a baked stuffed vegetable, salad, and homemade bread. Corn pudding is a bright yellow mound next to the stuffed vegetable on each plate.

>   2 cups sweet corn, frozen or steamed and cut from the cob
>   3/4 teaspoon sea salt
>   Freshly ground black pepper
>   3 eggs, lightly beaten
>   1 1/2 cups milk
>   Butter
>   Paprika

1. Mix together all the ingredients except the butter and paprika.
2. Pour the mixture into a buttered baking dish. Dot the top with butter and sprinkle with paprika.
3. Bake in a 350 degrees F oven for 45 minutes or until a knife inserted in the center comes out clean.

Yield: Serves 4

Millet Soufflé

If you're not used to cooking with millet, this is an ideal way to start. Millet adds a nuttiness and a grainy texture to an egg and cheese soufflé. It also adds stability: you don't even have to think about a millet soufflé falling. I've found that this dish is also good for introducing friends to vegetarian dinners. I serve it with ratatouille or with a big salad, and with homemade grainy bread.

2 to 3 cups cooked millet (1 cup uncooked)
1/2 teaspoon sea salt
Freshly ground black pepper
1/2 cup or more grated Cheddar cheese
2/3 cup milk
3 egg yolks
1/2 pound mushrooms, sliced and stir-fried in butter
3 egg whites

1. Cook the millet. (See Index)
2. Mix together all the ingredients except the egg whites.
3. Beat the egg whites until they form a stiff foam. Fold them very gently into the millet mixture, trying to keep as much of the foam as possible while still getting the egg whites evenly mixed.
4. Pour the mixture into a buttered baking dish.
5. Bake in a 350 degrees F oven for 30 minutes or until the center is firm.

Variations:
—Add extra egg whites if you have them left from making mayonnaise or ice cream.
—You can make this dish without souffléing it, and it's custardy rather than fluffy. Don't separate the eggs. Rather beat the 3 eggs together, then add them to the rest of the ingredients.

Yield: Serves 4

Grandma's Zucchini Casserole

A garden casserole, with zucchini, onions, green peppers, potatoes, and cheeses all baked in a tomato sauce. Sliced avocado is the perfect accompaniment.

Olive oil
2 big zucchini, sliced
2 medium onions, sliced
2 green peppers, diced
Pinch dried or fresh marjoram
2 cooked potatoes, diced with their skins on
1/2 pound cottage cheese
1/2 pound Cheddar cheese, grated
1/2 to 1 quart long-simmered tomato sauce (See pages 210-211)

1. Stir-fry the onions, peppers, and marjoram in a little olive oil. Add the zucchini slices and continue stir-frying until they're tender.
2. Remove from the heat and toss in the potato cubes. Stir in the cottage cheese.
3. Pour a little tomato sauce in a baking dish (or into individual au gratin dishes). Arrange the vegetable mixture in the sauce, poking down the zucchini slices so they lie flat.
4. Cover with tomato sauce, and sprinkle with a thick layer of grated Cheddar cheese. Sprinkle with homemade bread crumbs if you have them.
5. Bake in a 350 degrees F oven for about 30 minutes, or until the casserole is hot and bubbly.

Yield: Serves 4

Zucchini Boom

A delicious way to use zucchini when they start to explode in your garden.

2 huge zucchinis or 4 smaller ones
Stuffing:
    Butter
    3 or 4 medium onions, diced
    3 or more cloves garlic, mashed
    1 teaspoon thyme
    1 teaspoon dried basil or 1 tablespoon fresh
    1 teaspoon dried marjoram or 1 tablespoon fresh
    Zucchini pulp, chopped
    1 big handful raisins
    1 fresh tomato, diced
    2 cups fresh bread crumbs or cooked brown rice
    1 cup cooked soybeans or cooked soy flakes
    2 eggs
    Fresh parsley, minced
    Fresh chives, minced
    1 teaspoon sea salt
    Freshly ground black pepper
Topping:
    Cheddar cheese, grated
    Fresh chives, minced

1. Cut the zucchinis in half lengthwise, then scoop out the insides leaving a sturdy shell.
2. Stir-fry the onions and garlic in butter. Add the herbs, and fry them a minute, stirring constantly. Add the chopped zucchini pulp, the raisins, and the chopped tomato, and cook until the pulp is tender. Remove the pan from the heat, and mix in the remaining ingredients of the stuffing. Add salt and pepper to taste.
3. Arrange the zucchini shells in a lightly oiled baking dish. Line each shell with grated Cheddar cheese, then mound in stuffing.
4. Cover the shells with a thick layer of Cheddar cheese, and sprinkle with chopped chives.
5. Bake in a 350 degrees F oven for 40 to 50 minutes, or until the zucchini shells are tender.

Yield: Serves 4

Eggplant Parmigiane

Eggplant should be ripe. You can tell when it is ripe when there's no green near the stem. It should also feel light when you pick it up. Unripe eggplant is greenish, very firm, and dense.

This recipe is probably the most popular eggplant casserole. Eggplant slices are fried and then covered with tomato sauce and lots of cheese. Make a big, chaotic beautiful salad to go with the orderly stacks of eggplant. Serve homemade bread and butter and your favorite red wine. Eggplant parmigiane can be a durable down-to-earth dinner or a wedding feast.

> 2 medium eggplant, sliced
> Whole wheat flour
> Olive oil
> 1 quart long-simmered tomato sauce (See pages 210-211)
> 1 pound mozzarella cheese, grated
> Parmesan cheese, freshly grated

1. Cut the eggplant in slices 1/2 inch thick. Sprinkle the slices with salt and leave them 20 minutes. The salt will draw out some of the water so your slices won't be too juicy when you cook them. After 20 minutes, press the slices with your hand or under a plate to remove excess water.
2. Dredge each slice in whole wheat flour, then fry the floured slices on both sides in a little olive oil. Keep the heat under the frying pan fairly high, and the slices won't absorb as much oil. Fry the slices until they're lightly browned.
3. Arrange half the slices in a big casserole dish. Cover them with a sprinkling of mozzarella cheese. Top with the remaining eggplant slices.
4. Spread the casserole with tomato sauce, and cover with a thick layer of mozzarella and grated Parmesan cheese.
5. Bake in a 350 degrees F oven for about 40 minutes, or until the top is starting to turn golden. Let the eggplant parmigiane ripen for a few minutes after you take it out of the oven before serving it.

Variations:

—Cover the tomato sauce with thinly sliced onion rings or a layer of stir-fried mushrooms. Then cover them with the final cheese layer.

—Spread 1/4 cup of toasted sesame meal over each eggplant layer. Toasted sesame meal is roasted sesame seeds ground up in your grain mill.

—Spread lots of chopped black olives with the mozzarella cheese between the eggplant layers.

Yield: Serves 4 to 6

Moussaka

A vegetarian adaptation of a well-known Greek eggplant casserole. It has layers of fried eggplant, a red wine, mushroom, and grain layer, and a thick layer of seasoned white sauce.

With moussaka I serve Arabic bread, and a salad made from spinach, feta cheese, and black olives, dressed with olive oil, black pepper, and lemon juice. Drink Greek wine too.

> 2 medium eggplant, sliced
> Whole wheat flour
> Olive oil
> Butter
> 4 medium onions, diced
> 2 or 3 cloves garlic, mashed
> 1 bay leaf, chopped together with the garlic to make a fine paste
> 2 teaspoons oregano
> 1 teaspoon cinnamon
> 1/2 pound mushrooms, sliced
> 2 tomatoes, chopped, or 1 cup homemade tomato sauce
> 3 cups cooked brown rice, rye berries, or barley (1 cup uncooked)
> 1 cup red wine
> 1 quart whole wheat white sauce, with nutmeg and with 3 eggs added for thickening (See pages 214-215)
> Parmesan cheese, freshly grated

1. Prepare and fry the eggplant slices. (See eggplant parmigiane steps 1 and 2.)
2. In a saucepan stir-fry the onions in a mixture of butter and olive oil. Stir in the garlic-bay leaf paste, oregano, cinnamon, and mushrooms. Continue frying.
3. When the mushrooms are cooked, add the tomatoes or tomato sauce, the cooked brown rice, rye berries, or barley, and the red wine. Simmer the mixture for about 15 minutes or until it's thick. Taste for salt.
4. Arrange half the eggplant slices in the bottom of a well-buttered casserole dish. Spread with the rice and mushroom mixture. Cover with the remaining eggplant slices.

5. Pour whole wheat white sauce over the casserole, and sprinkle it with Parmesan cheese.

6. Bake in a 350 degrees F oven for about 45 minutes, or until the top white sauce layer is firm.

Variation:

—Mazouka—Make moussaka with zucchini instead of eggplant. Zucchini can be sliced and fried without pressing or dredging in flour.

Yield: Serves 6

Eggplant Manicotti

Manicotti filling rolled up in thin slices of eggplant is a very unusual treat.

    2 or 3 medium eggplant
    Filling:
        1 pound ricotta cheese
        1 pound mozzarella or Cheddar cheese, grated
        Good-sized lump Parmesan cheese, grated
        Lots of raisins
        2 eggs
        2 teaspoons cinnamon
        2 teaspoons dried rosemary, crushed
        1/2 teaspoon sea salt
        Lots of fresh parsley and scallions, finely minced
        Red wine
    3 to 4 cups long-simmered tomato sauce with 1 teaspoon dried
        rosemary (See pages 210-211)
    Mozzarella or Cheddar cheese, grated

1. Wash the eggplants; don't peel them. With a serrated bread knife, slice the eggplants *lengthwise* in slices 1/4 to 1/2 inch thick. The slices will be shaped like shoe soles. Steam the slices for about 8 to 10 minutes or until they're just flexible enough to roll. I steam eggplant in my pressure cooker without the pressure gauge.
2. Mix together the ingredients of the filling. Moisten it slightly with red wine.
3. Put a good heaping spoonful of filling in the center of each eggplant slice, and roll it up. Arrange the rolls in a buttered baking dish, pushing the rolls against each other so they'll stay rolled up.
4. Cover the rolls with tomato sauce, and sprinkle with a thick layer of mozzarella or Cheddar cheese.
5. Bake in a 350 degrees F oven for about 30 minutes, then turn off the oven and leave the casserole in to firm up.

Yield: Serves 6

Peanutty Eggplant

Stuff eggplant shells with stir-fried ginger, sherry, peanuts, and bread crumbs, then cover with a sherry white sauce. Serve with stir-fried green vegetables.

2 medium eggplant
Stuffing:
    Unrefined oil (Sesame or peanut is best.)
    4 medium onions, chopped
    2 green peppers, chopped
    2 or more teaspoons finely minced fresh ginger
    Eggplant pulp, chopped
    1 cup sherry
    2 cups peanuts, roasted in the oven
    2 cups fresh whole wheat bread crumbs
    4 eggs
    2 teaspoons sea salt
Topping:
    Whole wheat white sauce with a little sherry (See pages 214-215)

1. Slice the eggplants in half lengthwise and scoop out the insides.
2. Stir-fry the onions, green peppers, and ginger in unrefined oil. Add the chopped eggplant pulp and the sherry, and continue cooking until the eggplant is tender. Mix in the peanuts and cook a few minutes more. Remove from the heat, and mix in the remaining ingredients of the stuffing.
3. Arrange the eggplant shells in a lightly oiled baking dish. Press the stuffing into the shells in firm mounds.
4. Pour a thick coating of white sauce over the mounds.
5. Bake in a 350 degrees F oven for about 40 to 50 minutes, or until the eggplant shells are tender.

Yield: Serves 4

Mim's Turkish Eggplant

Lots of cinnamon, onions, pine nuts, and raisins, layered with white sauce. Similar to moussaka, but more exotic. Serve with evolution salad for a festive and colorful dinner.

    2 medium eggplant, sliced
    Whole wheat flour
    Olive oil
    4 medium onions, diced
    1/2 teaspoon cinnamon
    1 cup cooked brown rice
    Raisins
    Pine nuts or walnuts
    2 cups whole wheat white sauce with 1/2 teaspoon cinnamon

1. Prepare and fry the eggplant slices as for eggplant parmigiane steps 1 and 2.
2. Fry the onions in olive oil; mix in the cinnamon; and mix in the brown rice.
3. In a large baking dish, layer a few eggplant slices, then the onion mixture. Sprinkle generously with raisins and pine nuts. Continue layering this way, and end with an eggplant layer.
4. Pour white sauce over the casserole.
5. Bake in a 350 degrees F oven for about 30 minutes, or until the top of the casserole is browned and bubbly.

Variation:
—Use zucchini instead of eggplant.

Yield: Serves 4

Charlotte's Zapping Cabbage Packets

Do you think of stuffed cabbage as dull, dismal fare? Humbug!
This dish is an example of what you can do with herbs and spices.

    12 large cabbage leaves
    Stuffing:
        Butter
        2 medium onions, diced
        1 clove garlic, mashed
        1 teaspoon fennel seed
        1 teaspoon sage
        1 teaspoon paprika
        1/2 teaspoon dry mustard
        3 cups cooked millet (1 1/2 cup uncooked)
        2 eggs
        1 cup cottage cheese
        1 teaspoon sea salt
    Bed:
        2 cups sauerkraut
    Topping:
        1/2 quart home-canned tomatoes, mashed up
        1 cup sour cream (1/2 pint)
        Salt and pepper

1. Boil or steam the cabbage leaves about 10 minutes, or until
they're soft enough to roll.
2. Stir-fry the onions in butter. Mix in the other herbs and spices
and fry them a minute, stirring constantly. Remove the pan from
the heat and mix in the remaining ingredients of the filling.
3. Stuff the leaves: put a dollop of stuffing in the center, fold
in the sides, and roll up the leaf.
4. Make a bed of sauerkraut in a baking dish. Arrange the packets
in it, fold side down so they don't open during baking.
5. Mix together the ingredients of the topping. Add salt and
pepper to taste. Pour this sauce over the cabbage packets, and
sprinkle with paprika.
6. Bake in a 350 degrees F oven for about 40 minutes until hot.

Yield: Serves 4 to 6

Mom's Birthday Party Mushrooms

Lots of tasty cheesy morsels. Serve the mushrooms in steaming heaps, each plateful topped with a sweet red pepper ring or a bright red tomato slice.

> 2 pounds big mushrooms
> Stuffing:
>> Olive oil
>> Mushroom stems, chopped
>> 3 or 4 cloves garlic, mashed
>> 1 cup fresh whole wheat bread crumbs
>> 1/2 cup finely minced fresh parsley, scallions, or chives
>> 4 eggs, beaten
>> 1 cup ricotta cheese
>> Sea salt
>> Freshly ground black pepper
>> 1/4 cup freshly grated Parmesan cheese
>
> Topping:
>> Parmesan cheese
>> Paprika

1. Pull the mushroom stems out of their caps.
2. Chop up the mushroom stems and stir-fry them in olive oil. Stir in the garlic and fry it too. Remove the pan from the heat, and mix in the remaining ingredients of the stuffing. Add salt and pepper to taste.
3. Stuff each mushroom cap. Arrange the caps in a lightly oiled baking dish.
4. Sprinkle with Parmesan cheese and paprika.
5. Bake in a 350 degrees F oven for about 30 minutes, or until the mushrooms are tender.

Yield: Serves 4

Cheese & Walnut Stuffed Peppers

Serve with a salad, and with fresh corn-on-the-cob, cornbread, or
Tante Kathinka's corn pudding.

   6 big green peppers
   Stuffing:
     Butter
     4 medium onions, chopped
     2 cups cooked brown rice
     1 cup walnuts, chopped finely or run through a meat grinder
     1/2 pound Cheddar cheese, grated
     4 eggs, beaten
     2 teaspoons caraway seeds
     Sea salt

1. Prepare the peppers for stuffing by cutting out their stem caps
and removing the pulp and seeds.
2. Stir-fry the onions in butter. Put them in a large bowl, and mix
in all the other ingredients of the stuffing.
3. Stuff each pepper as full as it can be. Arrange the peppers open
end up in a baking dish. Pour a little water into the dish.
4. Bake in a 350 degrees F oven for 30 to 40 minutes, or until the
peppers are tender. (If you have any extra filling, bake it up
separately in a small oiled casserole for a side dish, or save it for a
main dish for another day.)

Yield: Serves 6

BAKED STUFFED VEGETABLES

Stuffings can be any grain and herb mixture. Use your cooked grains, cooked beans, or bread crumbs. Season them with herbs, onions, and lots of garlic. Bind them together with eggs, nuts, and cheese. Cover your stuffed vegetables with any of the sauces in the Sauces chapter.

To bake, arrange your stuffed vegetables in a lightly oiled baking dish. Pour the sauce over them. (If you're making baked stuffed eggplant, zucchini, or green peppers, and aren't using a juicy sauce, pour a little water or wine into the pan to keep them from drying out.) Bake the dish in a 350 degrees F oven for about thirty to forty minutes, or until the vegetable shells are tender and the stuffings are hot all the way through.

Eggplant
Cut the eggplant in half lengthwise, then scoop it out. Dice the insides and fry them up in the stuffing.

Zucchini
Prepare exactly as you would eggplant.

Green peppers
Cut in half, then scoop out the seeds. Or cut out the stem cap, scoop out the seeds, and stuff the whole peppers.

Mushrooms
Get large ones. Morels, which you can find growing wild in the spring, are ideal for stuffing. Pull the mushroom stems out of the caps. Dice the stems finely and fry them for the stuffing.

Onions
Boil the onions until they're just starting to be tender. Pull out the center sections, leaving a nice cavity.

Tomatoes
Scoop out the pulpy insides and stuff the tomato shells.

Potatoes
Bake potatoes, then slit them on the top and scoop out the insides. Mix them with sour cream, caraway seeds, chopped chives, or grated cheese. Stuff this mixture back in the skins, and bake until everything is hot again.

MEXICAN DISHES

Mexican meals taste best and look most authentic if they're served straight from the oven on piping hot plates. I like arranging individual servings of my main dish on ovenproof plates 'con arroz y frijoles' (with helpings of cooked rice and beans). I sprinkle everything with grated cheese, then pop the plates into the oven for about twenty minutes. When the cheese is melted and the food is hot, I add a dollop of sour cream, and rush the plates out to the guests at the table. Individual green salads topped with huge mounds of guacamole are a cool, crunchy accompaniment to the hot part of the meal. Beer is the best beverage to serve with Mexican food.

Recipes for special rice and bean side dishes follow.

Spanish Rice

Brown rice is sautéed in olive oil, then cooked up with tomatoes, green pepper, and onions. Serve as a side dish for Mexican meals, either in a big bowl or baked on the individual plates. Spanish rice can also be a main dish itself, served with cottage cheese and a salad.

Olive oil
2 or 3 cloves garlic, mashed
1 medium onion, chopped
1 green pepper, chopped
1 cup uncooked brown rice
2 cups water
1 teaspoon sea salt
1/2 quart home-canned tomatoes, or 2 fresh tomatoes, diced

1. In a medium pot, stir-fry the onion, green pepper, and garlic in olive oil. Stir in the rice and fry a few more minutes.
2. Add the water and salt, and bring to a boil.
3. Simmer, covered, about 35 minutes or until the rice is tender and most of the liquid is absorbed.
4. Stir in the tomatoes, and cook, uncovered, for another 15 minutes or until all the liquid is absorbed.

Yield: Side dish for 4 to 6

Refried Beans With Cheese

Delicious, with lots of cheese and onions. If you can find it, add epazote, an herb which enhances the bean flavor. Serve with Spanish rice as side dishes for Mexican meals, or use refried beans as a filling for enchiladas or as a layer in tostadas. A pot of warm refried beans is an excellent dip for crisp tortillas.

Butter
Cooked pinto or kidney beans, with cooking liquid
Onion, finely diced
Monterey jack or mild Cheddar cheese, grated
Epazote, dry or fresh

1. Melt butter in a cast iron pot. The more butter you use, the richer the beans will be.
2. Add cooked beans and liquid a little at a time, mashing them into the butter with a spoon or a potato masher. You can either mash the beans completely to a smooth paste or just mash a few to give the mixture body while leaving most of the beans whole.
3. Stir in the onion and a few sprigs of epazote. Then continue cooking and stirring until the mixture is quite thick. Again the thickness you aim for is a matter of personal preference.
4. Shortly before serving, mix in the cheese, and stir until it melts. Use as much cheese as you want for rich beans. Add salt to taste.

Variation:
—Add small cubes of cream cheese instead of the grated jack or Cheddar cheese.

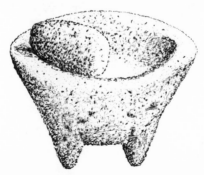

MEXICAN MORTAR & PESTLE—I grind garlic and spices, and mash avocados for guacamole.

Craig's Refried Beans

Spicy! Good for dips, burritos, omelette fillings, and on salads. Best if used right away, but refries do store well.

4 cups uncooked pinto or black beans
1 medium onion, chopped
1 large green pepper, chopped
1 bulb garlic, cloves peeled and mashed
1 teaspoon ground chiles or cayenne pepper
8 teaspoons ground cumin
4 teaspoons ground coriander
1 teaspoon black pepper
1 teaspoon oregano
1 teaspoon basil
1 teaspoon dill
4 teaspoons sea salt
(Optional: 1 tablespoon cumin seed, 1 teaspoon dried mustard, 8 drops tabasco)
1/2 cup butter (1/4 pound)

1. Cook the beans in 12 cups water until soft enough to mash—about 2 hours on top of the stove.
2. In a separate pan fry the onions, peppers, and garlic in oil until limp. Fry in all the herbs and spices for about 5 minutes. Add more oil if necessary to keep from sticking. (Frying brings out the flavor of spices.)
3. Mash the beans till smooth using a potato masher. Mix in the cooked vegetables and spices. Finally, mix in the butter.
4. Taste for salt.

Yield: Serves 6—8

Tostadas

A towering mound of beans, cheese, and salad piled on top of a flat crisp-fried tortilla. One or two tortillas are usually enough for each person.

Tortillas
Layers (from bottom to top):
  Refried beans or thick chili
  Grated cheese
  Shredded lettuce
  Red chile sauce, hot sauce, or strips of peeled green chile
  Marinated artichoke hearts
  Fresh tomato slices
  Sliced avocado or guacamole
  Sour cream
  Black olives

1. Get all your layer ingredients cooked, chopped up, and ready.
2. Prepare tortillas. Either fry them 1 at a time in a little hot oil until crisp, then drain them on a paper bag, or toast them until crisp on a dry skillet.
3. Pile layers on the fried tortillas. Either warm the beans in a pot so the hot beans will melt the cheese, or pop the tortillas under the broiler to melt the cheese over the beans. Then proceed layering.
4. Serve immediately. A big pot of hot refried beans is a good side dish.

Variations:
—The layers on your tostadas can be as diverse and as high as your imagination runs. See the list of enchilada filling ingredients for more ideas.
—Serve tostadas as a make-your-own buffet. Put the fried tortillas on one plate, and arrange ingredients for all the other layers in separate bowls. Keep the beans hot either in a double boiler or over a flame. Guests assemble their own mounds of food.

Enchiladas

Filled tortillas, covered with red chile sauce. The name of the dish comes from the sauce: 'enchilada' means 'in chile sauce.' Hot or mild, rich or light, enchiladas are a creative and delicious dish to serve for a regular meal or for company.

Tortillas or quick fake corn tortillas (See Index)
Filling
Red chile sauce (See pages 212-213)

1. Toast tortillas on a griddle until they're lightly browned.
2. Soften them by dipping the tortillas in warm chile sauce. Then either roll the tortillas around a filling, much like crêpes, or fold the the tortillas in half around a filling, or stack the tortillas with layers layers of filling between them. (All this can be done beforehand.)
3. Shortly before you're going to eat, cover the rolls or stacks of filled tortillas with red chile sauce. I usually arrange 2 or 3 filled tortillas on individual plates, spoon sauce over them, then put rice and beans on the plate and sprinkle everything with cheese. I bake the plates for about 20 minutes in a 350 degrees F oven. Or you can arrange all the filled tortillas in a baking dish, cover them with sauce, bake them, and serve them from the baking dish. Warning: Don't bake enchiladas too long or they'll dry out.
4. Before serving, garnish baked enchiladas with a dollop of sour cream or quacamole, chopped radishes, chopped scallions, or chopped black olives.

Enchilada Fillings

There is a wealth of foods to choose from. Use them alone or in combinations.

    Monterey jack, colby, or mild Cheddar cheese, grated
    Chopped onions or scallions
    Chopped black olives
    Refried beans
    Chopped hard-cooked eggs
    Cream cheese
    Sour cream (with fresh chives)
    Guacamole or sliced ripe avocado
    Chopped radishes
    Chopped fresh green pepper, either hot or sweet
    Marinated artichokes
    Raisins and almonds

My favorite fillings:

Grated cheese with chopped olives and chopped onion

Hard-cooked egg with cream cheese and lots of scallions

Guacamole with scallions. Put a dollop of guacamole on top right before serving.

Refried beans with onions and grated cheese

Steamed green peas with cream cheese and chopped fresh parsley and chives

Chile Rellenos

Stuffed fresh green chile peppers. My favorites are filled with Monterey jack or mild Cheddar cheese, cooked inside a puffy egg batter, omelette-style, then heated in the oven with red chile sauce.

The green chiles best for stuffing are a bright light green, about four to seven inches long, one to two inches in diameter at the stem end, and tapering to a point. Called anything from 'frying chiles' to 'Cubanelles' and 'California green chiles,' they're available all over the country. The thicker, meatier chiles are sweeter than the thin ones.

I'll give directions for preparing one chile relleno. Although it takes a lot of writing, the procedure is quite simple and satisfying as you watch it work. Plan on making one or two chile rellenos for each person, and multiply ingredients accordingly.

> 1 fresh green chile pepper
> A finger-size piece of Monterey jack or mild Cheddar cheese
> Batter:
> > 1 egg
> > 2 teaspoons whole wheat flour
> > Pinch of sea salt
>
> Red chile sauce (See pages 212-213)

1. Roast and peel your chiles. If you have an electric stove, toast the chiles on the rack under the broiler, turning the chiles frequently until they're browned and blistery all over. If you have a gas stove, toast the chiles directly in the flame of a burner until they're browned and blistery. Put the blistered chiles in a bowl of cold water, and leave them for about 5 minutes or until they're cool enough to handle. The skins will loosen during this cooling. Using a sharp knife, pull off the chile skins bit by bit. If any skin sticks, leave it on. It is not crucial to get off all the skin.

2. Lay each chile flat on a cutting board, and with a knife slit the chile about 2 inches starting from a little below the stem. Try to leave the area around the stem intact and the stem firmly attached. The stem gives you something to grab onto as you cook the chile, and also looks good. Remove the seeds and the core of the chile.

3. Insert a finger of cheese in the center of the chile, and close the edges of the chile around it. (This all can be done beforehand.)

4. Prepare the batter.
   a. Separate the egg.
   b. Beat the egg white until stiff.
   c. In a separate bowl, mix the yolk well with 2 teaspoons of whole wheat flour and a pinch of salt.
   d. Fold the yolk mixture gently into the beaten white.

5. Cook your stuffed chiles one at a time. In a buttered frying pan over medium heat, make an oval mound of half an egg's worth of batter. Lay a stuffed chile in the middle, and cover it with another half an egg's worth of batter. Cook it about 4 minutes, or until it's firm enough to flip, then turn it over and cook it for a few minutes on the other side until it's firm and golden-brown. Put it aside on a serving plate or in a baking dish, and continue cooking your remaining chiles.

6. Cover the chile rellenos with red chile suace, then bake them in a 350 degrees F oven for about 20 to 25 minutes to heat them through. I usually put the chiles on individual ovenproof serving plates, pour red chile sauce over them, then put helpings of rice and beans on the plates too. I sprinkle grated cheese over everything, pop the plates into the oven for about 20 minutes, then pull them out when we're ready to eat.

A green salad with a big mound of guacamole or bleu cheese dressing (sour cream mixed with bleu cheese and green herbs) is a good first course to serve while the chile rellenos, rice, and beans are heating.

Variation:
—Stuff the chiles with refried beans rather than with cheese.

Yield: 1 chile relleno

Tamale Pie

This pie is the best of both the grain and bean worlds: it's made from your homemade chili, topped with a thick cornmeal crust. Tamale pie can be made especially quickly is you have leftover chili on hand. See the Index for a recipe for cashew chili.

Tamale pie is even better reheated a second day, since the layers firm up overnight.

Crust:
    1 cup cornmeal
    3 cups water
    1 teaspoon sea salt
    2 or 3 eggs
Filling:
    4 cups thick homemade chili

1. Mix the water, cornmeal, and salt in a pot, and heat the mixture slowly to a boil, stirring constantly so it doesn't stick.
2. Simmer the mixture, stirring constantly, for about 5 to 10 minutes, or until it's good and thick, a hefty cornmeal mush. Remove it from the heat.
3. Beat the eggs in a bowl. Wisk in a little of the mush. Then mix it all back into the main bulk of the mush. Heat it for just a minute to firm up the eggs.
4. Spread the chili over the bottom of a lightly oiled baking dish. Spread the cornmeal mush evenly over that.
5. Bake the pie in a 350 degrees F oven for about 40 minutes, or until the crust is browned and firm.
6. Take the pie out of the oven and let it sit for 10 minutes before serving. This will allow the pie to solidify, and you'll be able to cut it neatly.

Variations:
—Add chopped black olives to the chili.
—Sprinkle the top of the pie with grated colby cheese.

Yield: Serves 4 to 6

CURRY

Curry is an Indian food. The spices used in it are mostly native to India and the East Indies, but the bite in curry, chile powder, reached India only after America was discovered. Native black pepper was used before that. As I was reading about the cumin and coriander, cinnamon and cloves that make up curry powder, it suddenly dawned on me that these regular old spices were what the 'spice trade' was all about. They were one reason why the Crusaders were so excited when they came back from the Holy Land, one reason why Columbus was trying to reach the Indies. A lot of history is motivated by our stomachs.

When I'm serving a curry dinner, I make a big hot curried vegetable dish (Anar's London curry). I make bright yellow cashew rice to go with it, cucumber raita to cool down everyone's mouth, and chappatis to use for bread and as pincers to pick up food. Then I fill little bowls with colorful and flavorful foods (sliced bananas, raisins, grated fresh coconut, grapes, peanuts, chopped hard-cooked eggs, almonds, avocado slices, and orange sections) to scatter around the main curry and make the display even more enticing.

Curry Powder—You Can't Go Wrong

Preground curry powders are stale and lifeless. I grind curry spices in a mortar and pestle or in my grain mill. Turmeric is essential. 'Once you have turmeric,' says my Indian friend Philip, 'You have curry. Add any other spices you wish. You can't go wrong.' Turmeric is a member of the ginger family, only yellower and more delicately flavored than ginger. Get whole dried turmeric root if possible and grind it.

    1 teaspoon ground turmeric
    1 teaspoon cumin seeds
    1 teaspoon coriander seeds
    4 or more whole cloves
    2 pods cardamon
    1 teaspoon or more chili powder or ground dried chile pepper

Grind up the seeds and mix the spices together.

Variations:
—The recipe above is a very basic curry powder. There are many other spices you can experiment with.

    Fenugreek—a deep chocolatey curry flavor
    Whole mustard seeds, toasted in a skillet
    Poppy seeds
    Cinnamon
    Allspice
    Nutmeg
    Asafoedita—a very strong-smelling resin. Use only a pinch.
    Black pepper

Yield: About 1 tablespoonful

Anar's London Curry

Indian friends in London showed me how to make this curry. It starts with sizzled onions, freshly ground curry spices, and tomatoes. You cook vegetables in this spicy base.

Butter
2 medium onions, diced
2 cloves garlic, mashed
1 teaspoon finely minced fresh ginger (or 1/2 teaspoon dry ginger only if you absolutely can't get fresh)
1 tablespoon basic curry powder, plus all the experimental spices you wish to add
1/2 to 1 quart home-canned tomatoes, or 3 to 8 fresh tomatoes, chopped
1 teaspoon sea salt
Vegetables (Choose from the curry vegetable list at the back of the section.)
Juice 1/2 lemon

1. Sizzle the onions in butter.
2. Add the garlic and ginger, and stir-fry some more, until the garlic is golden.
3. Add the curry powder, and fry it with the garlic and onions. Stir constantly. Be sure not to burn the powder. That's a mistake it's too easy to make if you're not on your guard. Add more butter if the spices start to stick.
4. Pour in the tomatoes and add sea salt. Simmer this mixture for about 30 minutes. (Use fewer tomatoes for a drier curry, more tomatoes for a juicy curry.)
5. Cut the vegetables you're currying into bite-sized pieces, and add them to the base to cook them. Add the vegetables which take longest to cook first. (See the curry vegetable chart.) As they cook, the curry spices penetrate the vegetables along with the tomato juice, adding a strange exciting flavor to each vegetable.

6. When the vegetables are done, add the lemon juice. Then ask a friend to taste the curry for seasoning. Your own taste buds will be blanked out after cooking the curry. More fresh lemon juice or more salt are common reseasoners. I never add more curry spices at this point. Unless they are fried at the beginning, they just taste raw.

7. Sprinkle the curry with finely chopped fresh coriander leaves if you can get them.

8. Serve the curry in its big pot, along with the rice, raita, chappatis, and all the side garnishes you've been arranging.

Variations:

—Add fruits to the cooking curry. Bananas, oranges, and pineapple are especially good.

—Add raisins, small chips of fresh coconut, or chopped nuts.

—Mix a little yoghurt into the finished curry to make it richer and milder.

Yield: Serves 4 to 6

Curry Vegetable Chart

**Long-cooking
vegetables:**

Tiny new potatoes,
   unpeeled
Big potatoes, unpeeled
Carrots
Broccoli
Cauliflower

**Medium-cooking
vegetables:**

Okra
Green beans
Eggplant (especially
   good with potatoes)

**Short-cooking
vegetables:**

Green peas

Bright Yellow Cashew Rice

Serve as a side dish with curries.

Butter
2 medium onions, diced
1 cup uncooked brown rice
1 teaspoon ground turmeric
2 cups water
1 teaspoon sea salt
1/2 cup cashews
4 or 5 scallions, chopped

1. In a medium pot, stir-fry the onion in butter. Stir in the rice and fry a few more minutes. Sprinkle in the ground turmeric, and stir it in quickly so it doesn't burn.
2. Add the water and salt, and bring slowly to a boil.
3. Simmer, covered, for about 35 minutes or until the rice is done.
4. Toss in the cashews and scallions right before serving.
5. Serve the rice in a big bowl, garnished with orange slices.

Yield: Side dish for 4 to 6

Chappatis

Whole wheat pancakes which you use as pincers to pick up curry, rice, yoghurt, and sprinklings. Then you somehow try to get them to your mouth. It's hard to be as graceful as the long-fingered Indians I have seen. This recipe makes twelve chappatis. You should count on having two or three chappatis for each person.

    2 cups whole wheat flour
    1 teaspoon sea salt
    3/4 cup (more or less) water
    Butter

1. Reserve a little flour for kneading, then mix the rest with the salt in a bowl. Add enough water to get a stiff dough.
2. Knead 5 to 10 minutes.
3. Cover the dough with a damp towel and leave it for 1/2 to 3 hours.
4. When everything else is almost ready for dinner, get out the dough. This is a last-minute operation, and from now on is performed most efficiently if 2 people are working. One kneads and rolls; the other fries.
5. Knead the dough again. Shape it into 12 balls. Knead each ball about 30 seconds, then roll it out with a rolling pin until it's a thin round. Roll it on a lightly floured counter, or on a counter covered with poppy seeds.
6. Heat a skillet over fairly high heat. Butter it lightly. Fry each chappati, flipping it once, until both sides are brown and puffy.
7. Brush the top of each chappati with melted butter. Stack them as they come out of the skillet, and keep the stack wrapped in a towel so the chappatis stay hot and soft until you serve them.

Variation:
—Poppy seed chappatis—Toast 1/4 cup of poppy seeds in a skillet. Add them to the flour along with the salt.

Yield: 12 chappatis

Cucumber Raita

A cooling yoghurt dish.

1 large cucumber or 2 small ones
2 cups plain yoghurt
1 teaspoon cumin seeds, toasted in a dry skillet
1/8 teaspoon cayenne pepper
1/8 teaspoon paprika
Fresh parsley, finely minced
1/4 teaspoon sea salt
Freshly ground black pepper

1. Grate the cucumber. Don't peel it.
2. Mix all the ingredients together. Adjust salt and pepper to taste.
3. Chill.

Variations:
—Add chopped fresh tomato.
—Add chopped cooked potato.

Yield: Side dish for 4 to 6

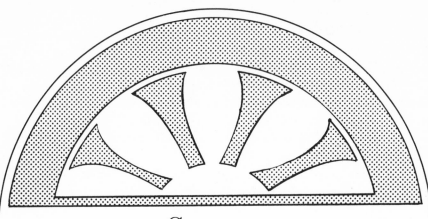

Sauces

Sauces add flavor to casseroles and juiciness to crêpes. Sauces give the body to stir-fried vegetables which makes them a filling main dish. Spicy sauces are the zing in Mexican food; tomato sauces make Italian dishes memorable. You can add your favorite herbs and spices to your sauces to create the exact taste you like.

Just-Cooked Tomato Sauce

A sauce with a zippy taste, more like fresh tomatoes than long-simmered tomato sauce. A treat on hot fettuccine. It's also the sauce I use for pizza.

    2 tablespoons olive oil
    2 cloves garlic, mashed
    1 teaspoon oregano
    1 quart home-canned tomatoes, or about 6 to 8 fist-sized fresh
        tomatoes, chopped
    Freshly ground black pepper
    1/2 to 1 teaspoon sea salt

1. Heat the olive oil in a heavy saucepan. In it stir-fry the garlic and oregano until the garlic is just turning golden. Stir constantly so nothing sticks.
2. Drain the juice from the home-canned tomatoes and save it for soup. (You don't cook this sauce long enough for the juice to evaporate.) Pour the canned or fresh tomatoes into the saucepan, and mash them with a wooden spoon to mix them with the garlic and oil, and to break them up a bit. Don't smash too much, since lumps of tomato are good in this sauce.
3. Grind in lots of coarse black pepper, and mix in the salt.
4. Heat the sauce, stirring constantly, until it's hot. This will only take about 5 minutes. If it's too juicy, cook it a bit longer to evaporate some water. Never put a cover on this sauce.

Yield: 3 cups

Long-Simmered Tomato Sauce

A deep-flavored tomato sauce, with onions, garlic, oregano, and red wine. You simmer it uncovered in a big saucepan until it's thick.

Olive oil
2 medium onions, diced
1 green pepper, diced
2 or more cloves garlic, mashed
1 teaspoon dried basil
1 teaspoon dried oregano
Pinch dried thyme
1 quart home-canned tomatoes, or 6 to 8 fist-sized fresh
    tomatoes, chopped
Freshly ground black pepper
1 bay leaf
1/2 teaspoon sea salt
A good pour red wine

1. Stir-fry the onions and green pepper in olive oil in a big saucepan. (I like using my cast iron soup pot.) Stir in the garlic, fry it a minute or 2, then stir in the herbs and fry them quickly.
2. Add the tomatoes, smashing them slightly so the sauce will be smooth. If you're using fresh tomatoes, cover the pot after you add them, lower the heat, and cook them 5 to 10 minutes so they juice.
3. Add the pepper, bay leaf, salt, and red wine.
4. Simmer the sauce for about 1 hour to thicken it and to blend all the flavors. Leave the pot uncovered so excess liquid can evaporate. Stir frequently so the sauce doesn't burn on the bottom of the pan.
5. Taste. Adjust salt and other seasonings.

Variations:

—Add finely minced fresh marjoram to the simmering sauce.

—Add a handful of raisins to the sauce to take away any bitterness from the tomatoes and herbs. A grated carrot has the same effect, but it's more subtle.

—Add a handful of pine nuts to give the sauce a fresh zing.

—Fry a pinch of cinnamon in with the onions and garlic.

—Fry just a tiny bit of hot red pepper, fresh or dried, in with the onions and green pepper.

—Stir-fry sliced fresh mushrooms in with the onions and green peppers.

Yield: 1 well-seasoned quart

Red Chile Sauce

A simple sauce, flavorful and fiery, based on large dried red chile peppers. You can cut the hotness by adding home-canned tomatoes, and can vary the taste by adding garlic, onions, and spices. Red chile sauce is used frequently in Mexican cooking. It keeps very well frozen, so you can make up a batch, freeze it in several small containers, and have it ready to use whenever you make Mexican meals.

Large dried red chiles are commonly available in the American Southwest, where they're called California, Anaheim, or New Mexico chiles. Different but similar varieties of chiles are called chile pasilla or chile ancho. The peppers are commonly strung in long braids called ristras. If you live on the East coast, you might be able to grow large hot peppers and dry them yourself, or you might be able to find dried chiles in a rare Mexican food store. However, if you don't have a ready supply, I'd suggest ordering chiles from Herman Valdez Fruit Stand, P. O. Box 25, Velarde, New Mexico 87582. They will mail you home-grown dried red chiles, either in a ristra, as loose pods, or ground into chile powder.

> 6 to 8 large dried red chiles (about 4 ounces)
> 3 cups boiling water
> 3 tablespoons butter
> 3 tablespoons whole wheat flour or cornmeal
> 1 teaspoon sea salt

1. Wash the chiles, then pour 3 cups of boiling water over them in a bowl. Leave them to soak until the water is cool, about 1/2 hour.
2. Pull off the chile stems. You may take out some of the seeds if you want a mild sauce, since the seeds are the hottest part of the chile. I like leaving all the seeds in.

3. Run the chiles, seeds and all, through a meat grinder, a Foley food mill, or your grain mill. (The grain mill makes the best purée, but you will have to take it apart and wash it after grinding the chiles.)
4. Mix the chile purée back into the soaking water.
5. In a large saucepan, melt the butter. Whisk in the flour or cornmeal. Gradually whisk in the chile purée. Add the salt.
6. Bring the mixture up to a slow bubble, then simmer it 10 minutes of until it's thick, stirring occasionally.
7. Taste. Add more salt if needed.

Variations:
—Toast the dried chiles on an ungreased griddle before soaking them. Watch them carefully so they brown but don't burn.
—If your sauce is too thick or is hotter than you like, after it's cooked stir in up to 1 quart of coarsely mashed home-canned tomatoes.
—Stir-fry 1 or 2 chopped onions in the butter before you add the flour.
—Stir-fry in the butter 2 or 3 cloves of garlic, mashed, or 1/2 teaspoon of either ground cumin or ground coriander. Add more to taste.
—If fresh coriander is available, sprinkle a few sprigs, finely minced, over the sauce just before it's finished cooking.
—If you don't have whole red chiles, you can make a reasonable red chile sauce using chili powder or ground dried chile peppers. Follow the recipe for long-simmered tomato sauce. In step 1, after you've stirred in the oregano, stir in

    1 tablespoon oil
    1/4 cup chili powder or ground dried chiles
    1 tablespoon ground cumin
    3 tablespoons whole wheat flour

Continue stirring to fry the chili powder quickly. Then stir in the tomatoes and proceed exactly as you would for tomato sauce.

Yield: 3 cups

Whole Wheat White Sauce

A medium-thick, all-purpose sauce with a creamy rich taste. Whole wheat flour doesn't lump, so your sauce will be smooth every time. This recipe makes about four cups of sauce.

    2 to 6 tablespoons butter or unrefined oil
    1/2 cup whole wheat flour
    4 cups milk (1 quart)
    1 teaspoon sea salt
    More salt and pepper to taste

1. Heat the butter or oil in a medium pot. The more oil or butter you use, the richer your sauce will be. Mix in the flour with a whisk.
2. When the oil and flour are blended, add the milk slowly, stirring vigorously with a whisk.
3. Bring the mixture to a bubble, then lower the heat and simmer it about 10 minutes. Stir frequently so nothing sticks. During this simmering the starch granules in the flour will loosen up and absorb water, causing the sauce to thicken.
4. Take the sauce off the heat, and stir in salt and pepper to taste. (A pinch of nutmeg is a very common ingredient in white sauce too.)

Variations:

—Most of the time you won't use basic white sauce, but will liven it up a bit. Following are suggestions, which you can use alone or in any combination with each other. (For more ideas consult any French cookbook.)

—Eggs for extra thickening: after step 4, beat up 2 eggs in a small bowl. Gradually add 1/2 cup of the hot cooked sauce to the eggs, whisking constantly. Pour the egg mixture back into the bulk of the sauce, and cook it 1 minute more, whisking all the time. The cooked egg will provide extra thickening.

—Cheese: after you take the sauce off the heat, whisk in grated Parmesan, provolone, or Cheddar cheese for a richer flavored sauce. Cheese sauces are delicious over cooked grains, pasta, or baked onions. They're also used in crêpes.

—Yoghurt or sour cream: for a smoother, more velvety sauce, whisk in 1/4 to 1/2 cup of yoghurt or sour cream after you take the sauce off the heat.

—Cream: add heavy cream to your white sauce after you take it off the heat.

—Mushrooms, shallots, and onions: slice these finely and sauté them in the butter when you start making the sauce. You might want to use a little extra butter. Then make the sauce right on top of the mushrooms or onions. (If you start this way, then add extra milk to your sauce, you'll have a cream soup.)

—Sherry: add a pour of sherry after you take the sauce off the heat. Red wine is good too. Don't add too much of either, or you'll curdle the sauce.

—Spices: nutmeg is good in any white sauce. Cinnamon is essential for Middle Eastern white sauces. Paprika reddens sauce. White pepper is spicier than black pepper, and is good when you don't want little black flecks in your sauce. Curry spices will give white sauce an exotic flavor. Serve a curry white sauce over cauliflower, cashew, and raisin stir-fries, or over rice. Ginger is good in white sauces for dishes containing peanuts. An Italian mixture of 4 spices is novel, and delicious in sauces for pasta. It contains white pepper, nutmeg, ground coriander, and ground juniper berries.

—Herbs: fresh tarragon white sauce is my favorite. I also like dill weed, parsley, summer savory, in fact any fresh or dried herb. (Broccoli stir-fried with walnuts, then served with a thyme white sauce is scrumptious.) Add herbs right after you put in the milk so their flavors cook through the whole sauce.

Yield: 1 quart

Charlotte's Master Sauce

A spicy Oriental sauce, with ginger, cinnamon, and star anise. Marinate vegetables in it before you stir-fry them, or soak dried mushrooms and bean threads in it. Use master sauce as liquid in your pan while you're making a stir-fry. Or heat up the sauce and pour it over a cooked stir-fry. Save the sauce and use it over and over. Always leave the spices and bits of vegetable caught in the sauce. Occasionally add more of the original ingredients. The sauce deepens with age.

    1/2 cup tamari sauce
    1 tablespoon honey
    2 tablespoons sherry
    1/2 cup water or vegetable water
    2 teaspoons sesame oil (Dark sesame oil is best.)
    2 cloves star anise
    1 clove garlic, mashed
    2 slices fresh ginger root, minced
    1/2 stick cinnamon
    1 or 2 scallions, minced

1. Mix all the ingredients together in a small saucepan.
2. Simmer some sliced carrots in the sauce to cook the sauce a little and take away the rawness. The carrots will be done in 25 minutes, and will be delicious.
3. Pour off the simmered sauce, and keep it in a jar in the refrigerator until you want to use it.

Yield: 1 1/2 cups

Sesame Onion Sauce

A medium-thick brown sauce with sweet cooked onions.
Particularly good over stir-fries with sliced zucchini or eggplant,
and over stir-fries with pasta.

    2 medium onions, sliced
    1/2 cup toasted sesame butter
    Juice 1/2 lemon
    1 teaspoon honey
    4 teaspoons tamari sauce
    1 cup milk

1. Cook the sliced onions in oil in a saucepan until they're
browned and sweet.
2. Take the pan off the heat. Stir in the sesame butter, lemon
juice, honey, and tamari sauce.
3. Slowly add the milk, stirring all the while.
4. Put the pan back on the heat. Simmer the sauce for 3 to 4
minutes to thicken it, stirring constantly.
5. Spoon the warm sauce over your stir-fry, or store it in the
refrigerator and heat it with a little more milk when you want to
use it.

Variation:
—Use peanut butter instead of sesame butter.

Yield: 2 cups

Karen's Honey Yoghurt Dressing

Spicy and slightly sweet. Serve over fruit or over fruit-filled crêpes.

    1 cup homemade yoghurt
    Freshly grated nutmeg
    Grated fresh ginger
    Few pinches cinnamon
    Grated rind and juice 1/2 lemon
    Honey

Mix together all the ingredients, and add honey to taste. Chill.

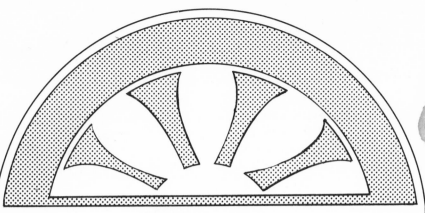

Desserts

Right after dinner I like a good mug of coffee with heavy cream. I make coffee fresh from well or spring water. I grind beans fresh. And I make filter or drip coffee—none of this perk nonsense.

Later in the evening I like dessert. My favorite desserts are simple and varied with the season. In the summer I like yoghurt sundaes with fresh fruits, berries, and maple syrup. In the winter I like dried fruits with cheese, wine, and nuts. And I must admit that I have a passion for ice cream at any time of the year. I especially like homemade ice cream, hand-churned in an ice cream freezer and eaten right away while it's still soft.

CONVERTING YOUR FAVORITE RECIPES TO NATURAL INGREDIENTS

Cookies and pie recipes are in general easily converted to natural ingredients. They will be darker colored and more flavorful. For pie crust, see the Index. Cakes are tricky. You can't make a butter cake recipe and substitute a liquid sweetening for the sugar. It won't work. In butter cakes, butter and sugar must be creamed together. This creaming beats in air which is essential to the texture of the cake. Oil cakes (zucchini cake, carrot cake, oatmeal cake, etc.) can be easily converted.

I look first at the sweetening in a dessert recipe. White sugar is out for nutritional reasons. Brown sugar is okay if it's real, but commercial brown sugar in this country is simply white sugar with a little molasses, artificial color, and artificial flavor added. The sweeteners I use are honey, maple syrup, molasses, and sorghum.

Honey is the most useful in making substitutions. (You can use a little molasses with the honey for a stronger-tasting, darker dessert.) But honey is sweeter per volume than sugar. Therefore you can't substitute honey for white sugar on a one-to-one basis. You will have to cut the quantity of honey down, say 3/4 cup of honey to 1 cup of sugar. You should also adjust the amount to your own taste—I prefer even less sweetening than 3/4 cup.

Since honey, maple syrup, sorghum, and molasses are liquids, you should cut down the liquid called for in the original recipe. If the recipe calls for 1 cup, cut it down to 3/4 of a cup. This will prevent your dessert from being dense and moist like pudding.

Desserts made with natural sweetenings will always brown more on the surface than desserts with sugar because of the chemical properties of the specific sugars they contain. To prevent excessive browning, I decrease the recommended oven temperature by 25 degrees F, and bake the dessert slightly longer.

For the fat in any recipe I use butter, not margarine. Sometimes I use tahini or peanut butter. In recipes calling for oil, I use a good-flavored unrefined oil. Peanut oil, sesame oil, and corn germ oil are especially good-tasting in baked goods. (I think dessert recipes are normally too rich as well as too sweet, so I cut back on the butter or oil called for.)

I prefer baking soda to baking powder, since most baking powders contain aluminum. When you use baking soda, you must add an acid food to react with the soda and produce carbon dioxide gas to leaven your dessert. (Baking powder doesn't require the addition of an acid; it contains a material which releases carbon dioxide.) For 1 teaspoon baking powder in a recipe, substitute 1/2 teaspoon baking soda plus 1 1/2 teaspoons lemon juice, or 1 1/2 teaspoons vinegar, or use 1/2 cup buttermilk in place of 1/2 cup regular milk in the recipe.

Whole wheat pastry flour substitutes nicely for white flour in all dessert recipes. Start out using an equal volume. Since whole wheat pastry flours vary in their protein content and thus in their ability to take up water, however, be prepared to add extra flour if your batter seems watery. Hard whole wheat flour (bread flour) can be used for cakes, cookies, and pies. It will make a tougher, more bready dessert.

Finally, I like to add lots of dried fruits and nuts to desserts. Rather than apologizing for natural ingredients, desserts can glory in them.

Stina's Apple Cake

You won't believe how good this is.

2 big apples
2 teaspoons cinnamon
2 cups whole wheat pastry flour
1 teaspoon baking soda
1/2 cup butter (1/4 pound)
3/4 cup honey
1/2 cup buttermilk
2 teaspoons pure vanilla extract

1. Slice the apples and mix them with the cinnamon. Set aside.
2. Mix the flour and baking soda. Using 2 forks or a pastry blender, cut the butter into the flour until the butter is in small pieces and evenly mixed.
3. Make a well in the center of the flour and butter, and in the well mix the honey, buttermilk, and vanilla. Mix them into the flour and butter, stirring just enough to combine.
4. Butter a 9 inch cast iron frying pan, or a 9 inch round deep cake pan. Put in some batter, then a layer of apples, then batter. Continue layering until everything is used up. End with batter on top. (Fill the pan only 2/3 full. If you have extra batter and apples, bake them in another pan.)
5. Bake in a 350 degrees F oven for 35 to 40 minutes, or until the center of the cake is firm.

Yield: 9 inch round cake

Banana Nut Tarta

A Swedish-style layered banana cake, topped with plenty of whipped cream.

    2 cups whole wheat pastry flour
    1 teaspoon baking soda
    1/2 cup butter (1/4 pound)
    3/4 cup honey
    1/2 cup buttermilk
    2 eggs
    1 teaspoon pure vanilla extract
    1 cup chopped walnuts
    3 bananas, mashed
    1 cup or more heavy cream (1/2 pint)

1. Mix the flour and baking soda. Using 2 forks or a pastry blender, cut the butter into the flour until the butter is in small pieces and evenly mixed.
2. Make a well in the center of the flour and butter, and in it mix the honey, buttermilk, eggs, and vanilla. Mix them into the flour and butter, stirring just enough to combine.
3. Mix in the walnuts.
4. Butter a 9 inch cast iron frying pan, or a 9 inch round deep cake pan. Pour in the batter. (Fill the pan only 2/3 full. If you have extra batter, bake it in another pan.)
5. Bake in a 350 degrees F oven for 35 to 40 minutes, or until the cake is well-browned on top and firm in the center.
6. Remove the cake from its pan and cool it.
7. Whip up the cream with a whisk. (Cream whips up best if it's cold.) Mix half the whipped cream with the mashed bananas.
8. Slice the cake in half to make 2 layers. Spread the banana-whipped cream mixture over the bottom half, and close it with the other half.
9. Spread the remaining whipped cream over the outside of the cake. Decorate with walnuts.

Variations:
—Mix strawberries with the bananas in the filling, or leave out the bananas and use just strawberries.

Yield: 9 inch round cake

Gingerbread

A moist and tender dark-black gingerbread which is very simple to make. Serve it with whipped cream or vanilla ice cream. Or serve it with a big bowl of yoghurt fruit salad for a summer dinner.

1/3 cup butter
3/4 cup molasses
1/4 cup honey
2 teaspoons baking soda
1/2 cup buttermilk
1 egg
1/2 teaspoon sea salt
2 teaspoons dry ginger
2 cups whole wheat pastry flour

1. Put the butter, molasses, and honey in a pot and cook until they boil.
2. Remove from the heat, add the baking soda, and beat vigorously with a wooden spoon.
3. Add the buttermilk and the egg. Then mix in the salt, ginger, and flour.
4. Pour the batter into an assortment of buttered pans, filling each about 2/3 full.
5. Bake in a 350 degrees F oven for about 15 minutes or until the centers of the cakes are firm.

Variation:
—Use whole wheat bread flour and add 1 cup of chopped raisins. This is more like bread, and is very good with Cheddar cheese.

Yield: Serves 6 to 8

Coconut Drops

Chewy, packed with fresh coconut and spiced with cardamon. Good with coffee.

1/2 cup butter (1/4 pound)
1 cup honey
1/2 teaspoon almond extract
Seeds from 2 pods cardamon, ground, or 1/2 teaspoon ground cardamon
2 cups or more freshly grated coconut
2 cups whole wheat pastry flour

1. Mix together the butter and honey until smooth. Add the almond extract, the ground cardamon, and the coconut.
2. Stir in the flour and mix until smooth.
3. Drop the batter onto buttered cookie sheets with a teaspoon.
4. Bake in a 325 degrees F oven for 25 minutes, or until the bottom of the cookies are lightly browned. The tops will be light, but firm.

Yield: 4 dozen

Maple Lace Cookies

A delicate oatmeal cookie, with the rich flavor of maple syrup.

1/2 cup butter (1/4 pound)
3/4 cup maple syrup
1 teaspoon pure vanilla extract
1/2 teaspoon sea salt
1 teaspoon baking soda
2 cups oat flakes (rolled oats)
1 1/2 cups whole wheat pastry flour

1. Beat the butter with a wooden spoon until smooth. Add the maple syrup and vanilla.
2. Mix in the salt and baking soda, then stir in the oat flakes. Stir in flour and mix until smooth.
3. Drop the batter onto buttered cookie sheets with a teaspoon. Leave the cookies plenty of room to spread out.
4. Bake in a 325 degrees F oven for about 15 minutes or until the cookies are firm. Let the cookies cool a few minutes on the trays to set before you remove them. Lace cookies have a very fragile texture.

Yield: 3 to 4 dozen

Sesame Cookies

Filled with the crunch of sesame seeds.

2 cups unhulled sesame seeds
3/4 cup peanut butter
1 1/2 cups honey
2 eggs
1 tablespoon lemon juice
1 teaspoon pure vanilla extract
1 teaspoon sea salt
2 teaspoons baking soda
3 cups whole wheat pastry flour

1. Toast the sesame seeds in a frying pan or in the oven until they're light brown.
2. Mix together the peanut butter and honey. Add the eggs, lemon juice, and vanilla. Mix in the sesame seeds.
3. Mix in the salt and baking soda, then stir in the flour and mix until smooth.
4. Drop the batter onto buttered cookie sheets with a teaspoon.
5. Bake in a 325 degrees F oven for about 15 to 17 minutes or until the tops of the cookies start to brown.

Yield: 5 to 6 dozen

Hermits

An orange, spicy fruit and nut cookie.

  1 cup tahini
  1 cup honey
  2 tablespoons molasses
  3 eggs
  Grated rind 2 oranges
  1 1/2 to 2 cups raisins
  1 1/2 to 2 cups chopped dates
  1 1/2 to 2 cups chopped walnuts
  1 teaspoon cinnamon
  1 teaspoon allspice
  1 teaspoon baking soda
  3 cups whole wheat pastry flour

1. Mix together the tahini, honey, and molasses. Add the eggs,
orange rind, dried fruits, and nuts.
2. Mix in the spices and baking soda, then stir in flour and mix
until smooth.
3. Drop the batter onto buttered cookie sheets with a teaspoon.
4. Bake in a 325 degrees F oven for about 15 minutes, or until the
tops of the cookies start to brown. (These cookies are best if
they're soft after they're baked.) Loosen the cookies from the pans
immediately after removing from the oven.

Yield: 5 to 6 dozen

Maple Apple Rice Pudding

Simple, wholesome, and surprisingly delicious. Serve it warm with cream or ice cream.

   2 cups cooked brown rice (3/4 cup uncooked)
   1/3 cup maple syrup
   1/2 cup chopped dried fruit (Figs are best.)
   2 or 3 medium apples, sliced
   Butter

1. Combine the rice and syrup. Add the chopped dried fruit and apples, and stir to mix.
2. Find a small casserole dish which has a lid. Butter it. Spoon in the rice mixture, and dot the top with butter.
3. Cover the dish, and bake in a 350 degrees F oven for about 40 minutes.

Variations:
—Try this pudding with other fruits, such as ripe peaches, plums, or pears.

Yield: Serves 4

Baked Honey Custard

This custard has a delicate honey flavor. Serve it cool: it tastes even better frosty cold than it does warm from the oven.

6 eggs
1/2 cup honey
1/2 teaspoon salt
4 cups milk
2 teaspoons pure vanilla extract

1. Whisk the eggs, honey, and salt together in a mixing bowl.
2. Heat the milk, and add it slowly to the egg mixture, whisking constantly.
3. Stir in the vanilla.
4. Pour the mixture into a casserole dish or into 8 individual custard cups.
5. Bake in a 350 degrees F oven for about 1 hour, or until the custard is firm and a knife inserted in the center comes out clean.

Variations:
—Sprinkle the top of the unbaked custard with freshly grated nutmeg.
—Mix grated fresh coconut into the unbaked custard.
—Drop slices of banana evenly over the unbaked custard. They'll float on top.

Yield: Serves 8

Honey Vanilla Ice Cream

To make homemade ice cream, you first make an egg and milk custard, then freeze it in a churn freezer. If you're buying one, the hand-cranked ice cream freezers are best, since you can vary the speed at which you're churning to make the smoothest ice cream. A five-quart freezer is a good size. In addition you'll need ice or snow to cool the freezer, and rock salt to help the ice.

    2 cups milk or light cream
    2/3 cup honey
    1/4 teaspoon sea salt
    4 egg yolks
    1/4 cup non-fat dry milk powder
    2 teaspoons pure vanilla extract
    1 cup heavy cream (1/2 pint)

1. Combine the milk, honey, and salt in the top of a double boiler. Heat the mixture to dissolve the honey, stirring every now and then.
2. Put the egg yolks in a small bowl and beat them lightly with a fork. Slowly add part of the warm milk mixture to the eggs, stirring constantly. Add this back to the main mixture. Sprinkle the dry milk over the mixture and stir it in.
3. Continue heating and stirring until the custard begins to thicken and will coat a spoon dipped into it.
4. Remove the inner metal container from your ice cream freezer, and pour the thick custard mixture into it. Cool it, either by putting it outside in the winter, or by resting it in ice water or putting it in the refrigerator in the summer.
5. When it's cool, add the vanilla and the cream.
6. To churn-freeze the custard, start by placing the container full of custard in the freezer tub.
7. Insert the dasher, adjust the cover, then attach the crank and lock it into position.
8. Make up an ice (or snow) and salt mixture. Make it 8:1 by volume, i.e. mix together 8 cups ice or snow to 1 cup rock salt. Fill the freezer tub with the mixture to a level about 1 inch below the cover of the inner custard container. Turn the crank occasionally to help pack the ice around the freezer.

9. Start to turn the crank, slowly at first and more rapidly as the freezing progresses. It's wise to have several people ready to churn, since the best ice cream is made with no pauses. As you churn, the water in the custard mixture freezes out in little crystals, mostly along the sides of the metal container where it is coldest. The dasher scrapes the crystals off the sides and breaks them up, making the ice cream smooth. Also the dasher beats air into the ice cream, so that it is creamy, rather than rock-hard and solid as it would be if it were still-frozen. As more and more water freezes out, the handle of the freezer becomes harder to turn. Don't slow the pace. If anything, speed up your churning so the ice cream will be smooth.

10. Continue churning until the mixture inside is firm. The crank will be very hard to turn at this point.

11. Unfasten the lock and remove the crank. Remove the metal cover. Dive in! It will never be better. (Some people repack the freezer top with ice-salt mixture, and leave the ice cream to ripen for about 30 minutes. I've never been able to wait.)

Variations:

—To make fruit and berry ice creams, add 2 cups of any mashed fruit or berry along with the heavy cream at step 5. Reduce the vanilla to 1 teaspoon. Taste the mixture before freezing it, since with less sweet fruits you may want to add extra honey. If you make banana ice cream, add the juice of 1 lemon.

Yield: 6 to 8 medium-size servings

Fresh Fruit Salads

I like eating individual fruits or berries. Sometimes I mix lots of fruits together, and serve them in my favorite bowls or in hollowed-out melon shells. I dollop yoghurt, yoghurt and maple syrup, or honey yoghurt dressing on top. (See Index)

Fruit cutting suggestions
Each fruit should be cut in pieces large enough that you can see the fruit's shape and color. However, each piece should be small enough to fit in your mouth.

Berries go in fruit salads whole.

Remove the membranes from grapefruit sections. (See Index)

Orange sections should be cut in half and deseeded. The luxury of eating fruit salad is ruined if you have to stop and spit out pits.

Apples and pears should not be peeled, but should be sliced so there is a bit of peel on each piece for color. Rub lemon juice on the cut surfaces to retard browning.

Grapes should be cut in half. Otherwise people tend to swallow them whole and miss out on that sweet squirt of grape juice. Again, seeds should come out.

Slice bananas.

Melons can be cut in slices, or can be made into balls with a melon baller.

Peaches, plums, and mangoes can be cut in slices.

Fresh pineapple is easiest to peel if you slice off the top and bottom, then cut into quarters lengthwise. Peel each wedge, and cut it into cubes.

Additions to fruit salads
With enough additions, a fruit salad can be a whole meal.

Toss some homemade yoghurt in with the fruit.

Squeeze oranges for juice if the salad seems dry.

Add chopped dates, figs, raisins, and other dried fruits.

Add cashews, almonds, walnuts, or shredded fresh coconut.

Add a little orange liqueur.

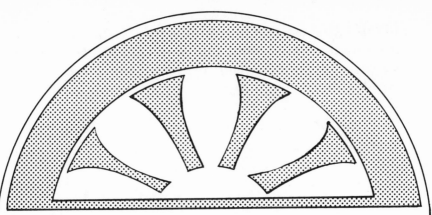

Odds & Ends

I like to make everything I possibly can from scratch. It's fascinating to see where foods come from—to watch beans turn into sprouts, to see milk solidify to yoghurt, to find that cucumbers have turned to pickles.

TOFU
SPINACH SOUFFLE

1 bunch fresh spinach
2 eggs, separated
8 oz. TOFU
1/2 cup yogurt or sour cream
Pepper to taste
Garlic powder to taste
Pinch of mace or nutmeg
1/4 cup grated Parmesan cheese
1/4 cup wheat germ

Preheat oven to 450 degrees F. Cook the spinach by steaming lightly, drain well, and set aside to cool. Combine egg yolks and TOFU and beat well. Add the yogurt and seasonings and mix thoroughly. In a separate bowl, beat the egg whites until they form stiff peaks. Chop the cooled spinach and blend it with the wheat germ and add the egg and TOFU mixture. Gently fold in egg - whites. Pour mixture into a lightly oiled casserole dish, top with grated cheese and extra wheat germ. Place in oven and immediately turn oven down to 350 degrees F. Bake for 1 hour, or until eggs are set and top is browned.

RECIPE SERVICE

rding to Persian tradition,
and to this food he owed
utritionally, yoghurt is only
s tangy taste and its
finitely a food worth the

You can vary its thickness
lk powder. For your starter
ny non-Swiss-style
ure has been killed in Swiss-
rt culture from a friend.

his makes the best yoghurt.
4 cups hot water. Don't worry
ve as the yoghurt forms.

oghurt from instant powder is not as
firm as yog...   tant powder. Make up 1 quart of
milk according to directions on the package. Add an additional
half cup powder: the extra protein and solids help firm the
yoghurt.

Fresh milk—Whole milk makes creamy yoghurt. Scald the milk to
kill any microorganisms which might compete with the yoghurt
culture and to alter the milk protein structure so it will coagulate
better. Scalding is especially important for raw milk, but even if
your milk is pasteurized, scalding will make a much firmer and
better-tasting yoghurt. While the milk is hot, mix in 1/2 cup of
dried milk per quart of fresh milk to increase the solids.

2. Pour the milk into a glass or crockery bowl. Never use a metal
container because the acid in the yoghurt might erode a metal
container.

3. Let the mixture cool to 110 degrees F. Use a thermometer to test the temperature, or apply the 'baby bottle test'—Milk is about 110 degrees F if it feels just slightly warm when you drip it on the underside of your wrist.

4. Stir in the yoghurt culture. It contains the bacteria *Lactobacillus bulgaricus* and *Streptococcus thermophilus* in a 1:1 ratio. The bacteria ferment lactose (milk sugar) to produce lactic acid. The acid causes the milk proteins to coagulate, giving you solid yoghurt.

5. Search out a warm spot. 110 degrees F is the ideal incubation temperature for yoghurt bacteria, but any temperature slightly above room temperature will do. Try over the pilot light of a gas stove, or in the oven if it has a pilot light. On a radiator, on a hot water heater, or on the furnace are good spots in the winter. Spots near wood-burning stoves are God's gift to yoghurt bacteria as well as to bread yeast. Or pour the mixture into a wide-mouth thermos bottle and close it. The thermos will keep the milk temperature exactly where you want it.

6. Cover the yoghurt bowl with a plate to keep out foreign particles, and leave it in the warm spot for at least 8 hours. I usually leave it overnight.

7. If the yoghurt hasn't solidified after 8 hours, leave it longer. Often yoghurt cultures are sluggish, especially on their first pass after coming from the commercial cup. Also, if the incubation temperature isn't high enough, it will take longer. But unless the culture is dead, if you leave the yoghurt long enough, something will happen. I wouldn't give up until a day has gone by.

After 1 day, if the milk tastes sour but still hasn't set up, put your bowl of yoghurt in the oven, and turn the oven on to its lowest temperature. Once the oven has come up to heat, turn it off and leave the yoghurt there for about 1 hour. Quite often this extra boost of heat is all the yoghurt needs to harden.

8. As soon as it is firm, put the yoghurt in the refrigerator to slow the bacteria and prevent the formation of excess acid.

9. Save 1/4 cup of this yoghurt to use as culture for your next batch of yoghurt. You can use the same culture for up to 7 or 8 passes before you have to buy new yoghurt. *L. bulgaricus* is stronger than *S. thermophilus*, so it gradually takes over and makes yoghurt harsher, more acid. If it were not for this, you could use the same culture forever.

What to do with yoghurt which fails to yoge:
What do you do with any good liquid? Make bread! Above all, don't be discouraged. Yoghurt cultures can be finicky. Get a new culture and try again.

Yoghurt which has yoged too long:
If you leave yoghurt in the warm spot for too long, the protein network which makes yoghurt solid will start to shrink and will squeeze out the liquid part of the milk—the whey. Some whey will always be squeezed out, but if you find a lot of whey on top of your yoghurt, you probably have overdone it. The yoghurt will still be good to eat, perhaps a bit tart. Just stir in the whey. But get a new culture for your next batch, and don't let it incubate for so long.

Variations:
—If you use more milk powder than I specify in the recipe, there will be more protein to give thicker yoghurt, and there will be some lactose left after the fermentation to give the yoghurt a sweeter taste.

Yield: 1 quart

Homemade Buttermilk

I often make buttermilk instead of yoghurt, since it's less fussy. Buttermilk bacteria 'go' at a lower temperature—about 72 degrees F (room temperature) rather than 110 degrees F. Buttermilk bacteria produce a more subtle flavor than the straight acid of yoghurt, so you get a milder, more smooth-flavored product. And buttermilk isn't quite as thick as yoghurt. I like drinking buttermilk, using it on granola, and I substitute it for yoghurt in cooking. Buy commercial buttermilk for a culture.

    1/4 cup buttermilk
    1 quart milk

1. Fresh whole milk makes the best-tasting buttermilk. Take it out of the refrigerator and let it warm to room temperature. (Do not add extra dry milk powder as for yoghurt.) Mix up dried milk powders according to directions on the package, and let them cool to room temperature.
2. Add 1/4 cup commercial buttermilk or 1/4 cup from your previous batch of buttermilk.
3. Leave it overnight at room temperature, and in the morning it should be set. If not, leave it longer. The longer you leave it at room temperature, the thicker it will get.
4. Store buttermilk in the refrigerator.

Variation:
—Sour cream is simply cream made acid by a buttermilk culture. Mix 2 tablespoons of homemade buttermilk with 1 cup of heavy cream, and leave it out at room temperature overnight.

Yield: 1 quart

Tofu (Soybean Curd)

I'd once thought tofu to be the exclusive property of Chinese restaurants, but now I find homemade tofu adding an exciting texture to vegetable stir-fries everywhere. I have tried to make it without using a blender, but I must admit defeat. I have not been able to grind the soybeans fine enough by hand.

  1 cup dry soybeans
  Water
  2 teaspoons Epsom salts

1. Soak the soybeans in water overnight.
2. The next day, divide the soaked beans in 4 parts, and mix each part with about 3 cups of water. Blend each in a blender until it's smooth. You now have soy milk.
3. Strain the milk through cheesecloth. Save the pulp left in the cloth to add to your next batch of bread.
4. Pour the strained milk into a large pot. Bring it up to a low boil, and simmer 3 minutes. Turn off the heat.
5. Dissolve the Epsom salts in 1/4 cup warm water. Stir this into the hot soy milk. Stop stirring. The mixture will start to curdle. The Epsom salts destabilize the protein in the soy milk, and cause it to precipitate out as a curd. This procedure is called 'salting out' the protein. (Epsom salts is named after the village of Epsom in England, which has a water supply with special laxative and wound-healing properties. Epsom salts is the substance formed after evaporation of the water.)
6. Wait 5 to 10 minutes, or until the soy milk is well-curdled. Using a big spoon or slotted spoon, lift the curd gently into a strainer lined with cheesecloth.
7. Press the curd down a little, then put another bowl on top of the curd as a weight. Leave it to press for a few hours.
8. If you don't use the curd right away, store it in the refrigerator. Use it within a few days, however, or it will lose its freshness.

Yield: Enough for a meal for 4

Sprouts

Inside a seed is all the material for a new plant. When you give it a warm temperature and water, the tiny embryo in the seed germinates and starts to grow. It bursts out of its seed coat, and sends forth a little shoot, which is the sprout. Sprouts are living food. Besides tasting fresh, crunchy, and often sweet, sprouts are a good source of Vitamin C, since the sprouting process converts some of the starch in the seed to Vitamin C. This is especially useful during the winter, when other good sources of Vitamin C can be hard to find. I use sprouts in salads, bread, and vegetable stir-fries.

You cannot sprout split peas because they're only half a seed. And don't sprout seeds you buy to plant in the garden because many of them are treated with chemicals to keep them from spoiling. However you can sprout whole wheat berries, whole lentils, Indian corn kernels, unshelled sunflower seeds.... My favorite sprouts are made from alfalfa seeds, mung beans, and fenugreek seeds.

1. Put the dried seeds or beans in a jar. (A clip-top canning jar is good.) Fill the jar only about 1/6 full of seeds, since the seeds will sprout up to many times their original volume. Fill the jar half full with lukewarm water, set the lid on loosely, and leave the jar out at room temperature for the seeds to soak overnight. Each seed will swell up with water, and the water absorbed by the tiny embryo will start its cells dividing.

2. Sometime the next day, drain off any extra water by pouring the seeds out into a strainer. Catch the water and save it for soup stock or for making bread. This first soaking water contains water-soluble vitamins from the seeds.

3. Rinse the seeds with fresh lukewarm water, as if they're being showered by a light spring rain. Put them back in the jar. They'll be slightly damp.

4. Set the jar lid on loosely again. Put the jar in a warm, dark spot, similar to the sprouts' home if they were growing in the earth.

5. Leave them until the next day.

6. Again turn the seeds out into the strainer, and shower them with water. Pour off the water, and put the seeds back in the jar.

7. Repeat the showering procedure once or twice a day for the next few days, or until the sprouts are a nice size. Mung bean sprouts are ready when the sprout is about 1 inch long. Alfalfa sprouts get longer and longer, until you could almost get tangled up in them. When they're about 1 1/2 inches long, put the sprout jar out in the sunlight for about 1 hour, and the sun will green the sprouts. Most beans, such as soybeans, should be sprouted for only 3 or 4 days. The beans will go rotten if you try for the really long sprouts they look capable of growing. The time your sprouts take will vary with how big the original seed was, how warm your sprouting place is, and how long you want the sprouts. But nature is wonderful. You start out with dry, hard seeds, and you end up with crunchy watery sprouts.

8. Sprouts are best if you eat them right after you make them. But if you store them in the refrigerator, they'll stay fresh for about 1 week.

Herb Vinegars

When you find a good red wine vinegar, get a large amount of it to make herb vinegars. They're a good way to save some of the fresh taste of summer herbs for winter salads.

Red wine vinegar
Fresh herbs (alone or combined):
  Basil
  Tarragon
  Mint
  Dill
  Marjoram
  Rosemary
  Garlic
  Shallots
  Horseradish

1. Cram the fresh herb leaves into a jar, or cover the bottom of the jar with finely minced solid herbs (garlic, etc.).
2. Fill the jar with vinegar.
3. Cover the jar and leave it at room temperature away from the sun for about a week or 2. Shake it every day.
4. Pour the vinegar off the herbs into bottles. Stopper the bottles. And the vinegar is ready to use.

Homemade Sauerkraut

A good way to preserve cabbages for winter eating. Shred cabbage, mix it with salt, and allow the bacteria naturally present on the cabbage to ferment it and produce the zingy sauerkraut taste.

Cabbages
Salt

1. Weigh the cabbages. Then shred them up evenly, in medium-size pieces. The cabbage shrinks as it becomes sauerkraut, so you don't have to shred it as finely as you would for cole slaw.
2. To make the best sauerkraut, put the shredded cabbage in a big plastic bag. I usually hate plastic bags, but they do keep air out. You can also make sauerkraut without the bag by putting the shredded cabbage in an open crock. However, it's been my experience that the sauerkraut goes moldy.
3. Measure 2 teaspoons salt for each pound of cabbage you started with. (1 cup = 16 tablespoons = 48 teaspoons) With your hands mix the salt into the cabbage. Be sure to get the salt evenly distributed, or the sauerkraut will ferment unevenly.
4. Twist the bag shut and fasten it securely. Put that bag into another bag, and ease the pouch into a big crock. The walls of the crock will lessen the pressure on the bags so they don't break. If you aren't using plastic bags, weight the top of the cabbage in the crock with a plate and a brick.
5. Keep the crock at cellar temperature—about 60 to 65 degrees F.
6. The sauerkraut will be ready in about 4 to 6 weeks. (If it's fermented at a higher temperature, it will be ready sooner; at a lower temperature it will take longer.) Taste the sauerkraut to determine when it's done.
7. Leave the sauerkraut in the bags and take out some as you want to use it. Most of the flavor is in the juice, so be sure to get some juice along with the cabbage. Boil the sauerkraut for about 10 minutes in an open pot before you use it. This destroys any toxins which might have been produced by microorganisms in the sauerkraut. It's highly unlikely that anything bad would have grown because normally sauerkraut is too acid for bacteria. However, if you boil it you can be absolutely sure you'll have no problems.

Granny's Kosher Dill Pickles

Crunchy, and flavored with fresh dill, garlic, and pickling spice. I like making them in a crock.

Small to medium-sized cucumbers, freshly picked
Garlic cloves, peeled
Fresh dill
Mixed pickling spice
Brine:
1/4 cup salt
1/2 cup vinegar, cider or white
1 quart water

1. Cut up 2 or 3 cloves of garlic into a crock. Add 1 teaspoon of pickling spice and about 1 handful of fresh dill.
2. Arrange a layer of cucumbers. Use them whole, since if you cut them up, they become mushy. Sprinkle the cucumbers with a few pieces of fresh dill and 1/2 teaspoon of pickling spice. Continue layering cucumbers and spices in this way.
3. After the final layer of cucumbers, cut up a few more cloves of garlic and put them on top. Add 1 more teaspoon pickling spice and a final handful of fresh dill.
4. Make the brine. Multiply the ingredients in the recipe above to make sufficient brine to cover the cucumbers.
    a. Boil salt and water.
    b. Add vinegar.
    c. Pour over cucumbers while still boiling.
(You need vinegar to make the brine acid. This guarantees no undesirable organisms will grow in the pickles.)
5. Set a plate weighted with a brick on top of the cucumbers to keep them under the brine.
6. Leave the crock at room temperature for the cucumbers to ferment. The pickle flavor comes from lactic acid, which the bacteria naturally present on the cucumbers produce by fermenting the sugars in the cucumbers.
7. The pickles will be ready to eat in about 2 weeks. Leave them in the crock, and take them out as you want to eat them. They'll be good all winter.

Pickles in a gallon jar (a commercial-size mustard or mayonnaise jar):
Make pickles exactly as you would in a crock, but instead of weighting everything with a plate and a brick, wedge the cucumbers into the jar so they're covered with brine. The important thing is to keep the cucumbers under brine. Put the lid on the jar, and leave the cucumbers'to ferment.

Pickles in quart canning jars:
A good way of packing small batches of pickles. Also, pickles packed this way stay slightly crisper than pickles made in a crock. The procedure is a miniature version of the crock procedure.

1. Put a few cloves of garlic, 1 teaspoon pickling spice, and a small handful of fresh dill on the bottom of each jar.
2. Stick the cucumbers lengthwise into the jars.
3. Make brine, and pour it over the cucumbers to cover them.
4. Close each jar with the appropriate canning lid. (The lids on pickle jars aren't for a tight vacuum seal, as with canned tomatoes, for instance, but only for a cover. There is no need to process pickle jars in a boiling water bath to seal them.)

Home-Canned Tomatoes

Home-canned tomatoes are the staple of my cooking. Can all the tomatoes you can get. I guarantee you'll use every jar you put up.

A tomato canner is just a very big pot. You do not need to use a fancy pressure canner for tomatoes, since they're acid enough to be safe canned at normal water boiling temperature. (New varieties of low-acid yellow tomatoes do require a pressure canner. I think they're tasteless and would never use them anyway, however.)

Canning equipment:
  Canner
  A medium-size pot to scald tomatoes in
  A metal colander or a big strainer to fit into the scalding pot
  A sink full of cold water
  Paring knife
  Canning jars
  Canning jar lids
Ingredients:
  Ripe tomatoes
  Sea salt
Optional ingredients:
  Garlic cloves, peeled
  Fresh parsley sprigs
  Fresh basil sprigs

1. Get all your equipment together. Assemble canning jars during the year. Usually there's no need to buy new ones, since so many old jars would love to be filled up. Use last year's jars. Buy some at auctions. Mayonnaise jars are perfect for canning: they have the right-sized neck for normal canning lids. Ask friends to save jars for you. Several other companies are making jars which can be used for canning. Check peanut butter and yoghurt jars especially. Buy jar lids or jar rings to fit your jars. If you don't have a canner, borrow one from a neighbor, buy a second-hand one at an auction or in a shop, or buy a new canner in a hardware store.

2. Pick tomatoes. It's fine to pick tomatoes as they ripen and hold them for a day or 2 until you can accumulate enough to can a batch. You can fit 7 quart jars at a time in a normal canner, and about 1/3 bushel of tomatoes will fill 7 jars. Judge when you're ready.

3. On the day you're going to can, check jars to make sure the edges aren't chipped. Chips let in air and the jars won't seal properly. Discard chipped jars (or store grains in them). Wash good jars in warm water. Rinse them well, and turn them upside down to drip out.

4. Wash jar tops—rings and lids. Put them in a pot of water so you can heat and sterilize them when you're ready to use them.

5. Rinse the tomatoes to get the garden dirt off them.

6. Now all the organizing is out of the way, and the real canning process begins. First, scald the tomatoes so you can peel them. Fill the scalding pot about half full of water and bring it to a boil. Fill the colander or strainer with tomatoes, and lower it into the water. Be sure the water covers all the tomatoes. Let the water come back to a boil, then pull out the colander. Dump the scalded tomatoes immediately into a sink of cold water. The boiling water will have loosened the tomato skins, and the cold water will cool the tomato quickly so you can slip the skins off. Let the water in the pot come back to a boil, then plunk in the next load of tomatoes.

If 2 of you are canning, one can start peeling tomatoes and stuffing them into canning jars, while the other continues scalding. If you're canning alone, you have to move more quickly to carry on both operations at once.

7. Turn the clean canning jars right-side up. Put 1 teaspoon of salt in each quart jar; 1/2 teaspoon in each pint jar. You can also put a peeled clove of garlic, a sprig of fresh parsley, or a fresh basil leaf into each jar for extra flavor.

8. Peel the scalded tomatoes, and stuff them into the jars. To peel, cut out the stem scar in a small cone with a paring knife. Pull on the skin, and it should slip right off. If a skin sticks, try scalding the next batch of tomatoes a little longer. The exact scalding time is something you can work out as you go along. It's not crucial. Cram each jar full to within 1/2 inch of the top. Later, when the tomatoes are heated in the canner, they'll expand to fill this head space. Work the blade of a knife down the sides of the filled jars to remove entrapped air.

9. When you've filled enough jars to fill your canner, wipe off the tops of the jars carefully with a clean cloth. They will not seal unless the tops are clean. Boil the potful of rings and lids to sterilize them. Lift them out with tongs, and put them on the jars. Put rubber rings on jars that use them, and clip on their dome tops. Fit metal lids on jars that require them, then twist screw tops around to hold the metal lids in place.

10. Put the jars in warm water in the canner. Pour in enough warm water to cover the tops of the jars. Warning: Don't put the jars into very hot or boiling water because they will crack. Bring the water in the canner slowly to a boil.

11. Boil quart jars of tomatoes 45 minutes; pint jars 35 minutes. Boiling destroys any microorganisms which might grow in the tomatoes and spoil them during storage. Tomatoes are boiled for a shorter time than most other vegetables, and can be boiled at the lower tamperature of an open canner rather than the high temperature of a pressure canner because they're a high-acid food. Microorganisms die most quickly when they're heated in a high-acid medium.

12. Lift the jars out of the canner and set them in an undisturbed place to cool. (If you have another batch of filled tomato jars ready to can, add some cool water to that in the canner before you put the new jars in.)

13. As the tomatoes you've canned cool, they'll contract, forming a slight vacuum which pulls down the lids and seals them. With metal lids, you'll hear pops as the seals take and the lid centers are sucked down. Sealing is not as dramatic with rubber rings. Check each jar to make sure it's sealed. Wait until the morning after you've canned the tomatoes so the jars are completely cool. Pull rubber rings, and pry jar lids with your fingernail. If either comes off easily, the jar is not sealed properly. If a jar isn't sealed, wipe off its top. Check to be sure it's not chipped. If the jar is good, put a new lid on it, and boil it for another 35 minutes in the canner. If the jar is bad, transfer the tomatoes to a good jar, and process it in the canner. (I usually wait on these second tries until I can fill the rest of the canner with new jars of tomatoes.) If a jarful doesn't seal the second time around, eat the tomatoes or make them into soup or tomato sauce.

COFFEE GRINDER—I grind coffee beans fresh.

Index

This is the second in a series of Crossing Cookbooks.
The first is "The Long & The Short of Chinese Cooking"
by James Rollband. A manual for beginning cooks, it
"takes the terror out of Chinese cooking" (Publishers Weekly).
The third in the series is "The Melting Pot—The Variety of
American Ethnic Cooking" by Maria Gitin. Over 270 recipes:
Chinese, Hungarian, Jewish, Japanese, African, so on. The
variety that makes American cooking a wonderful melting
pot is all here.